SAN FERNANDO CATHEDRAL

For George and Marilyn,

In friendship,

Tim

D1511202

Timothy Matovina
May 2001

SAN FERNANDO CATHEDRAL

Soul of the City

Virgilio P. Elizondo
Timothy M. Matovina

ORBIS BOOKS
Maryknoll, New York 10545

Copyright ©1998 by Virgilio Elizondo and Timothy Matovina

Published by Orbis Books, Maryknoll, NY 10545-0308
Manufactured in the United States of America

Scripture quotations are from the New American Bible with Revised New Testament, copyright © 1986 by the Confraternity of Christian Doctrine.

Library of Congress Cataloging-in-Publication Data

Elizondo, Virgilio P.
   San Fernando Cathedral : soul of the city / Virgilio P. Elizondo,
Timothy M. Matovina
     p. cm.
   ISBN 1-57075-217-6 (pbk.)
   1. San Fernando Cathedral (San Antonio, Tex.)—History.   2. San Antonio
(Tex.)—Church history.   I. Matovina, Timothy M., 1955– .
II. Title.
BX4603.S49E45   1998
282'.764351—dc21   98-47101
                                                 CIP

CONTENTS

ACKNOWLEDGMENTS

Our colleagues at the Mexican American Cultural Center (MACC) participated in this project with untiring dedication. We thank especially Maria Elena González, Jane Hotstream, Rudy Vela, Janie Dillard, Lupe Ruiz, Marc Hinojosa, Enedina P. Cardona, Rosendo Urrabazo, Rosa María Icaza, Roberto Piña, and Juan Alfaro. The San Fernando study would not have been possible without their willingness to serve as consultants, organize meetings and conferences, facilitate discussions, conduct vital research, and, in a thousand other ways, offer assistance and time from their busy schedules. Although officially retired from his distinguished teaching career at MACC, John Linskens gave us inspiring guidance on this project, especially in the sections that deal with scripture. Jacques Audinet, professor emeritus at the Sorbonne and a long-standing MACC collaborator, offered an incredible breakthrough on the manuscript schema as well as his usual friendship and encouragement. Our students at MACC, the University of California at Santa Barbara, Princeton University, and Loyola Marymount University contributed their enthusiastic responses and helpful critique at various stages of the project's development.

We are also grateful to the Lilly Endowment for supporting this study and for providing us the opportunity to deepen our working relationship and friendship. In particular, we thank Olga Villa Parra, whose vision, ingenuity, and wisdom helped create this project and sustained it at every step of the way. Similarly, James P. Wind and Carol Johnston have consistently accompanied and inspired us; Jim also honored us by writing the insightful foreword to this volume. The expertise and encouragement of Endowment directors Craig Dykstra and Jeanne Knoerle further enhanced our efforts.

Numerous scholars, San Fernando staff and congregants, and other people associated with the cathedral guided our study through the

viii ACKNOWLEDGMENTS

various consultations that comprised it. Pamela Ilott graciously received us for consultations at her retreat center on Canyon Lake, providing a place of reflection and conversation and enriching our deliberations with her wealth of knowledge and experience. Our conversation partners included experts in congregational studies, pastoral ministry, communication arts, spirituality, ethnography, community activism, Latina/o religion, psychology, business, politics, journalism, liturgy, popular faith expressions, advertising, religion and society, history, mission studies, religious video, theology, culture, anthropology, and ritual studies. Their lively exchanges with San Fernando parishioners and staff, with one another, and with us provided many of the ideas presented in this work. While their names are too numerous to mention individually, we are deeply grateful to each one.

Lionel and Kathy Sosa and their associates designed the cover for this book. Their fascination with San Fernando and its people is evident in the work of art that they created. Lionel and Kathy Sosa and Gene Martínez provided the original photographs used for the cover. The photographs inside the book are from James and Donna Schaffer, Janie Dillard, Gene Martínez, Felipa Peña, Manuel Medellin, Ruben Alfaro, Ralph González, and the Institute of Texan Cultures at San Antonio. Our colleagues Janie Dillard and Lupe Ruiz helped select the illustrations and obtain the necessary permissions. David García, the current cathedral rector, wrote a moving afterword that clearly illuminates the ongoing development and transforming power of the San Fernando congregation and its ritual traditions. The staff at Orbis Books, particularly Susan Perry, did an outstanding job editing the book and seeing it through to publication. We gratefully acknowledge the contributions of these collaborators and thank them for helping us tell the San Fernando story.

Above all, we thank the people of San Fernando who have animated our faith and theological reflection. To them and their ancestors and descendants, we gratefully dedicate this book.

Virgilio P. Elizondo
Timothy M. Matovina

FOREWORD

I will never forget my first visit to San Fernando Cathedral. Colleagues had told me about the old adobe and stone church building, about its distinctive Mexican-American history, about its special public role in the city of San Antonio, about its deeply faithful people, and about its dynamic rector. So I was prepared to be impressed.

But in another sense, I was unprepared for that first visit. From the moment in December 1992 when I stepped into the nave of this, the oldest cathedral in the United States, I was encountering a reality that, for me at least, was very new. San Fernando was a cathedral unlike any other I had seen. It was smaller, simpler, older than all of North America's cathedral churches. This was a place where a different language prevailed, where a different history lived, where different saints and different celebrations shaped the daily lives of people. It was a place where, above all, a special kind of hospitality was offered to all. Later in my visit, when I joined hundreds of people in the crowded cathedral and, thanks to the satellites of Univision, millions of people around the world in an evening of serenades to Our Lady of Guadalupe, I knew that I was participating simultaneously in both part of the great past of American religion and part of its great future. I also recognized that I had entered a living mystery that would not let go of my imagination.

Those who have visited San Fernando Cathedral before will find that this book takes them on a wonderful return trip to this special American congregation. They will find themselves marveling once more at the cultural negotiations taking place here between the two Americas, one of Mexican, Tejano, or even Aztec origins, and the other Anglo or Northern European in background. They will confront again the riddles of this sacred place, with its long history in which first New Spain, then Mexico, then the Republic of Texas, and

finally the United States flew their flags over the central city plazas
that lie right outside the cathedral doors. They will be pulled back
into the mystery and power of the great traditions that merge and
harmonize there.

I trust that many who pick up this little book will be having their
first encounter with this special place and people. For all too long,
San Fernando Cathedral has been a secret well kept by those who
worship there, by those who know the city of San Antonio, or who
specialize in the history of North American Catholicism. Virgilio
Elizondo and Timothy Matovina, who were my hosts in 1992 and are
your hosts now, want to change that. They know that there is a great
story here, one full of drama, power, oppression, suffering, endurance, and creativity. They will take you further into the soul of San
Antonio and into the interiority of this Roman Catholic community
of faith than you might imagine can be done in such a brief
encounter.

Readers, whether newcomers or repeat visitors to San Fernando,
should prepare themselves for easy-to-read but difficult-to-grasp
chapters in which they learn about the ways that some Americans
have disempowered others, about how a city can be taken away from
its original owners and then centuries later returned (at least partially) to them. But this book is about more, so much more, than this
painful truth. The power of tradition is manifest here—both in its
local and in its transnational forms. The "great tradition" of Roman
Catholicism survives the centuries here, but it does so by joining in a
fascinating dance with the more particular, grounded "little tradition" that Mexican Americans kept alive in this one special place. In
fact, it is the power and life to be found in the dance of traditions and
cultures, what the authors call *mestizaje*, which is one of the central
discoveries or gifts that San Fernando, and Elizondo and Matovina on
its behalf, have to share with those of us who stop in for a visit.

Many who read this book will be leaders—lay and clergy—of congregations and parishes very different from the one described here.
Others will be scholars of religion, bringing different kinds of academic interests on their journey to San Fernando. To assist both groups,
I wish to provide the briefest of travel guides.

The first thing to notice about this book is that it is part of a growing literature called "congregational studies." That phrase, with its

Protestant provenance, has become shorthand, a kind of academic catch-all, for an interdisciplinary body of work that has focused on local assemblies or faith communities. Father Elizondo and Professor Matovina take their places as part of a growing cohort of people who are trying to understand these indispensable local communities of faith. But here it is very important to note the distinct new contribution made to the field by these authors. Elizondo and Matovina have pioneered a new kind of inquiry. As historian, Matovina probes the long history of San Fernando; by paying attention to rituals and practices he identifies a distinct cathedral tradition that he traces over the centuries. As priest/theologian, Elizondo reads the current rituals and practices of a faith community and finds a fresh, powerful, local theology embedded in the life of this particular community of faith.

This attention to ritual and liturgy, what faithful people do in their homes, in the streets of the city, and in the sanctuary is a wonderful addition to the many sociological and anthropological studies of congregations done in the past two decades. In essence, the authors have chosen another path into the life of a community of faith and invited us to see what can be learned by following it. This path opens vistas for us, places where we are offered—a rarity in current congregational studies—a priestly, pastoral interpretation of the life of a congregation. By and large the voices of congregational studies have been the voices of scholars, outsiders who come in to study and learn. Often seeking to become participant-observers, these scholars have brought fresh eyes to the familiar and have helped us see additional dimensions of congregational life. Unfortunately, the voices of astute insiders who read the congregation from within its practice and life have been missing from the field. This book steps into that gap. To be sure, Elizondo and Matovina are not just any insiders. As they relate in the pages that follow, Elizondo is a home-grown San Antonian with a long history of associations with the cathedral. He writes as one who has grown up with this place, served as its rector, and led the cathedral into a powerful time of recovery and reinvention of its traditions of public ritual. But Elizondo is also a world-renowned theologian, one who has studied with great theologians in places like Paris, the Philippines, Rome, and Medellín. So while he writes from inside the life of this congregation, he also writes as a person who brings much from the outside world. Matovina, who is of Irish Croatian background, went to San Antonio to study the history of Tejano people. San Fernando became one special place to study, but for him it also became a community of faith where he was more than an observer. As he indicates in the first chapter, he became a full participant in San Antonio's life, an insider, although a very different kind from most who gather at the cathedral.

I am certain that this book will set off debates within the current field of congregational studies, within certain theological circles, and among clergy about the strengths and weaknesses of this distinctive approach to the life of a congregation. Those debates about method, stance, point of view, and the like can only enrich each of those communities. It is clear, however, that this book pays attention to dimensions of congregational life that other studies have not always done justice to. The faces of people at prayer; the notes written and left at the feet of statues; the music the people sing; the local festivals and street rituals of a congregation; the sermons; catechetical instruction; the way a building becomes at different times of the year a stable, nursery, garden, cemetery, dining room; the testimony of homeless people and actors in religious pageants—these are the primary material brought into view by this phenomenological and theological approach. This way of looking at and interpreting a congregation seeks to take us deep into the interiority of one community of faith. The authors describe this way of working as "an attempt to discern the God who is alive in us." They also see this book as a counterbalance to the habitual presupposition on the part of too many religious leaders that the members of their parishes are ignorant, mistaken, and faithless. They ask us to take seriously the *sensus fidelium*, the living reality of faith in the life of a congregation.

Many other highlights await the reader on this journey into the life of a cathedral. I dare mention only one more. This book began out of a conversation at the Lilly Endowment on the significance of public rituals. Olga Villa Parra, who at that time was a colleague down the hall from me at the Endowment, introduced me to San Fernando Cathedral and its rector. She believed that a very special kind of public ritual was taking place in San Antonio that had significance for "cathedral churches" around the country. She was right. As one ponders the *posadas* and Good Friday processions through the streets of San Antonio described here, it is impossible to avoid questions about the absence of such public ritual from the lives of most congregations in this country. Elizondo and Matovina are not insisting that every congregation do exactly what San Fernando does. But they bear witness to a possibility of public drama and engagement, of worship that seeks to draw not just the converted or the pious into participation in great mysteries. In so doing they confront those of us with responsibilities for the worship life of congregations with questions and new possibilities. They challenge us to uncork our imaginations and see what can be done to engage the public in the substance of our congregational life.

It is time to place you in the hands of your hosts, the authors. Virgilio Elizondo and Timothy Matovina were my hosts on that first visit six years ago. I have returned many times and on each occasion encountered what Father Elizondo describes as the key characteristic of the people of San Fernando—hospitality. You are about to be welcomed into their world and given many gifts. Such encounters make us want to visit again and again. They also open our eyes and free us to change our ways and grow in faith.

James P. Wind
The Alban Institute

SAN FERNANDO CATHEDRAL

1

EXPLORING THE LIVING FAITH
OF A PEOPLE

Timothy M. Matovina and Virgilio P. Elizondo

In two recent articles in the *New York Times*, San Fernando Cathedral
has been referred to as "the heart of San Antonio" and "a place of
miracles." For anyone who enters for the first time, or anyone who
has been coming regularly to San Fernando for a lifetime, there is a
mystery, a magic, and an aura that cannot be explained in the statues,
the *milagritos* (little silver arms, legs, hearts, and so on) offered for
favors granted, the vigil lights everywhere, the plastic flowers in tin
cans, the stained glass windows, the street wino asleep, the distressed
man lost in prayer, the mother who prays in ecstasy beside her rest-
less children, the bank executive in deep meditation, the tourist in
outlandish attire, the very personal notes left with the Black Christ,
the early pre-dawn Mass that begins the day, the fiesta Sunday
Masses, the public rituals, the massive processions around the plaza.
Even the stone and adobe walls of this ancient sanctuary seem alive
with the memories they contain and the graces they emit. At San
Fernando, there is an immediate experience of a profound, dynamic,
living, loving, welcoming, alluring, listening, caring, and compassionate God who does not have to be explained. God's overwhelming
presence is immediately obvious.

This study explores the living faith of the San Fernando congregation. It stems from an ongoing conversation between Virgilio
Elizondo, a Mexican American who served as rector of San Fernando
from 1983 to 1995, and Timothy Matovina, an Irish Croatian American parishioner. We enjoy working together and find that our "insider" and "outsider" perspectives enhance one another. Our collabora-
tive effort draws on our study and discussions of theology, culture,

anthropology, ritual studies, and history. In addition to our friendship and these common interests, the genesis of the San Fernando project is our distinct but mutually enriching experience of this fascinating cathedral congregation.

A PARISHIONER'S EXPERIENCE

I became a parishioner at San Fernando Cathedral in 1992, when I relocated to San Antonio during the final year of working on my doctoral dissertation. My dissertation was a study of religion and ethnicity among nineteenth-century San Fernando parishioners, a study that enhanced my attraction to a faith community that fascinated me both personally and professionally. A year later, when Virgilio Elizondo, the cathedral rector, asked me to be his partner in a study of the San Fernando congregation, I eagerly accepted his invitation. The San Fernando congregation was already familiar to me because of my friendship with Father Elizondo. I had worshiped at San Fernando during previous visits to San Antonio; I had also marveled from a distance at the cathedral's international television ministry, particularly the weekly Sunday Mass and the annual broadcast of the *serenata* (serenade) to Our Lady of Guadalupe.

One of my most vivid first impressions as a San Fernando parishioner was of a *levantada del niño* celebration. The *levantada del niño* tradition (literally "taking up the child") entails a solemn removal of the child Jesus from the nativity scene, marking the end of the Christmas season. Family and friends gather at home for this ritual to venerate the infant Jesus with songs, prayers, symbolic gestures, and a meal or other festive gathering.

Esther, a lifelong parishioner whom I met shortly after arriving at San Fernando, invited me to the *levantada* celebration at the home of her friends Jesús and Emily, along with some sixty to eighty neighbors, relatives, friends, and fellow parishioners. When we arrived at our hosts' home we joined other guests in the living room in offering a silent prayer at a *nacimiento* (nativity scene) decorated with colorful *serapes*, poinsettias, other flowers, and Christmas lights.

This *nacimiento* extended along three walls of the living room and was like none I had ever seen. The usual cast of characters was there, of course: the magi with their camels and precious gifts, the shepherds and their flocks, the angels announcing the good news, Mary and Joseph, and the infant Jesus. But this image of Jesus was striking in that it was out of proportion to the other figures, a life-size baby large enough to hold and cuddle. What most caught my attention, however, were other characters, persons I recognized from the infancy narratives of Matthew and Luke but had never seen depicted in nativity scenes. Elizabeth reached out with open arms to embrace her kinswoman Mary. Simeon looked with wonder at the child in his arms while the prophetess Anna raised her eyes and voiced her thanks to God. Jesus' *abuelos* (grandparents), Joachim and Ann, were also there, visible reminders that he had elders and loved ones who rejoiced at his birth and concerned themselves with his well-being.

Other figures recalled the harsh and brutal events connected to the story of Jesus' coming among us. A Roman official held an opened scroll and barked out Caesar Augustus' command that all residents return to their place of origin and register for the census. One of Herod's soldiers stood with a bloody sword over an anguished mother who embraced the murdered body of her son. Mary and Joseph hastened on the flight to Egypt, Joseph looking back over his shoulder and scanning the horizon for signs of unwanted pursuers.

No one offered an explanation of why all these figures were included in the manger scene. No explanation was needed. Clearly this was not the sanitized version of the Christmas story to which I was accustomed, but the scandalous, unedited, full biblical account of the Savior's birth. My senses easily imagined the arrogance of Caesar Augustus, the jealous rage of Herod, the blind and brutal obedience of his soldiers, the uncontrollable tears of the mothers of the Hebrew innocents, the fear of the refugees Mary and Joseph, the sisterhood of Elizabeth and Mary, the wisdom of Anna and Simeon, the pride and concern of Ann and Joachim at their grandson's birth.

I was still soaking in the meaning of these vivid images when our hosts asked us to find our places for the *levantada*. We began the ritual by singing about half a dozen hymns together. Then we prayed the rosary. Five members of our group each led a decade of the rosary, interspersing prayers, songs, and scripture readings according to their own inspiration and taste. Next a reader announced the infancy narrative from Luke ("She gave birth to her first-born son and

wrapped him in swaddling clothes and laid him in a manger, because there was no room for them in the place where travelers lodged") and invited us to offer "testimonies" from the Christmas season. Group members offered various narrations, most of them accounts of how God had helped them or spoken to them during Christmas time: a healing from illness, a reconciliation within the family, children grasping the "true meaning" of Christmas, a family reunited for the holidays. These testimonies were followed by prayers of thanks and petition, again focused primarily on the immediate concerns and needs of those present.

After numerous participants had offered their prayers, we sang more hymns as each one of us silently stepped to the crib and venerated the child Jesus. Young and old alike honored the baby in the manger; adults placed the hands of infant children on the forehead or foot of the baby Jesus, tracing the sign of the cross or whispering some words of explanation. One by one, each person reverenced the babe in his or her own way: touching, caressing, smiling, bowing, holding, kissing, entreating. Our hosts gave candies to the guests after they had offered their homage to the child, a practice that my friend Esther told me "represented the sweetness of having Jesus in our life." The guitar, accordion, and voices provided a festive backdrop, but all eyes remained focused on the individual devotees as each had a moment of intimacy with the child.

When my turn came, I knelt and gently kissed the babe. At that moment I had the sensation that Jesus and I were alone and that he was there to hear whatever thought or concern I might express. No words came, just a feeling of gratitude for the sense of God's willingness to come near me. After the remaining devotees had processed to the manger and offered their gestures of homage, our hosts reverently lifted the Jesus image from the scene and removed it to a back room, out of sight from all. As if on cue, this action ended our singing and all remained in silence until our hosts returned to us.

The final act of this ritual was a teaching given by a long-standing San Fernando parishioner named Zulema. Zulema explained that she had been a Roman Catholic all her life and had accepted Jesus Christ as her savior, detailing the numerous ways that she had encountered Christ in her life and the life of her family. She went on to say that many San Fernando parishioners celebrated the *levantada* in their homes during this holy season and that we were participants in a sacred tradition that spanned generations.

Although Father Elizondo was not with us at the Salazar home for this *levantada* celebration, his presence was evident in the number of times Zulema quoted him and in the approving nods of her listeners whenever she mentioned his name. Zulema echoed Father Elizondo's message that Mexican Catholic traditions like the *levantada* were a treasure entrusted to us by our forebears. She also said that it was Father Elizondo who helped her to see that such faith expressions had served her people as a "living Bible" and "living gospel" for generations. Even her ancestors who could not read had the scriptures clearly opened to them through their participation in these sacred rituals. It was a night to thank God for the rich heritage we had received, not in silver or gold, but in the treasured expressions of faith handed on to us by our ancestors. For centuries these faith expressions had enabled the people to know Jesus, God's greatest gift to each one of us.

Later, when I met Zulema in her home for a private interview, I discovered that her convictions about Mexican Catholic faith expressions were long-standing. She recounted that her mother-in-law, Julia, first introduced her to San Fernando. Julia, who had six sons in World War II, kept an image of St. Anthony to whom she prayed for their safety. She made a solemn promise that if her sons returned from the war in good health she would offer their combined weight in wax for candles at the cathedral. It took her until 1949 to fulfill her promise, but she did it because she was "a woman of great faith." Zulema told me that she frequently repeats this account to young people and others at the cathedral because "we need these traditions to evangelize our children."

I have learned much from the San Fernando congregation about the significance of liturgy and ritual, public devotion and prayer. At San Fernando, rites like the *levantada* celebration awaken in people the powerful forces of memory and imagination. As Zulema clearly articulated, the *levantada* is a faith expression that unites contemporary devotees with one another and with the living memory of their ancestors. At the same time, the *levantada* enables participants to remember all the events associated with Jesus' birth. No shocking detail is omitted from the vivid depictions, which can easily jar newcomers like myself into recalling both the wonder and the horror that together comprise the story of Jesus' coming among us.

But this is not merely a nostalgic recollection of things past. As I worshiped with the others at the *levantada* celebration, the memory of momentous events in the life of Jesus stirred my imagination and led me to envision a world in which refugees overcome a wicked ruler bent on destroying them, a world in which evil directed at this world's innocents is not ultimately victorious, and a world in which God brings goodness out of sin and corruption. On the personal level, the *levantada* offered me a sensual encounter with an approachable God who takes on the vulnerability of a child and expresses unconditional love in the tenderness of a newborn babe. In this and many other instances, San Fernando's public rituals have ignited my imagination by bringing the gospel memory of Jesus to life in tangible, flesh-and-blood, dramatic, festive celebrations.

These ritual celebrations have also deepened my reflection on the scriptures. The *levantada* rite at Jesús and Emily's home forever altered my understanding of the infancy narratives. Never again can I read these texts without recalling the faces of Elizabeth, Simeon, Anna, Joachim and Ann, the Roman official announcing the census, Herod's soldiers, the mothers of the Hebrew innocents, Mary and Joseph on the flight to Egypt. Never again can I gloss over the indifference and the vicious cruelty that surrounded the scene of God's taking on our flesh. While I was previously aware of the callousness and the violence connected to the Christmas story, the unforgettable images of the *levantada* impressed on me just how completely God took on our human condition in the incredible scandal of the incarnation. The birth of Jesus is not disconnected from the harsh world I see on the daily news but is the ultimate sign of God's unbounded desire to enter in and become part of that world.

A PASTOR'S EXPERIENCE

San Fernando has always had a very special place in my life. It has always been the venerable center of our city; it is the place where my parents were married. I have vivid memories of serving Mass there as a young boy. Because Father Angel was a diabetic, he could only take a drop of wine and would leave the rest for the altar boys. As he ended the preface of the Mass with the traditional "With the angels and the archangels we sing the hymn of unending glory," the voice of Doña Regina would resound through the cathedral as she led the "Santo." She was one of the black-veiled venerable *viejitas*, the faithful custodians of our temple. She was often nicely accompanied by the snores of my grandfather, Don Antonio.

Meanwhile the sound of coins dropping into the vigil light offering box sounded like small church bells calling our attention to another liturgy going on spontaneously on the side. At the same time in another corner of the church, another faithful custodian meticulously arranged the paper flowers around the altar of the Blessed Mother. And always, somewhere in the church, unbothered by everything else that was going on, someone else was deep in meditation and prayer, completely undisturbed by the Mass. Outside, all around the church yard, there was life in abundance! Tacos, tamales, and *raspa* cones, *yerbabuena* and *nopalitos*, religious articles and flowers were for sale. People visited with each other, and children played everywhere.

My earliest memories of church were those of *Cristo Rey* (Christ the King) in our barrio. They retain a sense of excitement, togetherness, fascination, fun, music, and contemplation. There is no doubt that our parish church was God's family home for everyone to enjoy. Our God was incredibly ordinary, likable, and fun-loving. Although we loved our parish church, we were drawn to the breathtaking cathedral with its paintings, statues, beautiful architecture, and crowds of people. You were never alone. Once you walked into San Fernando, it became a part of you. There was no need to register as a parishioner, as there is no need for a baby to register as a member of the family that gives it birth.

As a Mexican American growing up in San Antonio, the Alamo was never anything more than a nice tourist spot, an extension of our school playground at downtown St. Joseph's Academy. It was the cathedral, a short distance away, that was the unquestioned sacred center of the city, the pulsating heart of San Antonio that kept the city alive and allowed it to prosper. It stood majestically in the center of the city, a quiet witness to everyday traffic and the events of the city and also to the movement of generations of peoples and of nations.

Later, while doing my doctoral studies in France during the late

1970s, I became fascinated with Europe's Gothic cathedrals and their role in building the great cities that emerged during the twelfth and thirteenth centuries. Old and majestic and incredibly alive with tourists, people at prayer, and ceremonies, the stones themselves seem to chant hymns of praise to God and to humanity's ingenuity. These cathedrals gave me a profound experience of the sacramentality of building cathedrals in the very center of the secular centers of life. Standing in the center of the great cities, they remind everyone that it is the task of men and women to transform their city into the city of God. This image of what a cathedral could mean for a city would later become key to my pastoral plan for San Fernando.

Another striking impression I had was that the cathedrals did not appear to be centers of dogma controlling the human mind, but rather flint rocks that could spark human beings into unimagined greatness and creativity. The great cathedrals of the twelfth and thirteenth centuries were a triumph of the imagination over the known architectural and theological sciences. They celebrated the illumination provided to humanity through the light of God. The world was not to be hated and feared. Men and women were not to fear the darkness and the unknown, but to celebrate the light. The cathedral placed God at the very center of all the activities of the city and elevated all the activities of the city to God, creating a unity in all the affairs of life.

I saw how cathedral sculptures recreated the imagery of the entire Bible. Centuries before the printing press and mass literacy, the cathedrals opened all the pages of the Bible and made them easily accessible to everyone. Even the most illiterate could come to know and appreciate the mysteries of the Word of God. The entire biblical adventure, from creation to apocalypse, was carefully recreated, interpreted, and illustrated by artistic imagination enlightened by faith.

Despite such experiences, for the years after I finished seminary I hardly ever thought of San Fernando. It was there, but my mind and work were elsewhere. Then, in 1983, the archbishop of San Antonio offered me a totally unsuspected opportunity, a position as rector of the cathedral. Immediately, my heart started to spin with memories, ideas, possibilities, and dreams. The archbishop had been working with me at the Mexican American Cultural Center (MACC) in San Antonio where our team of scholars and pastoral ministers explored

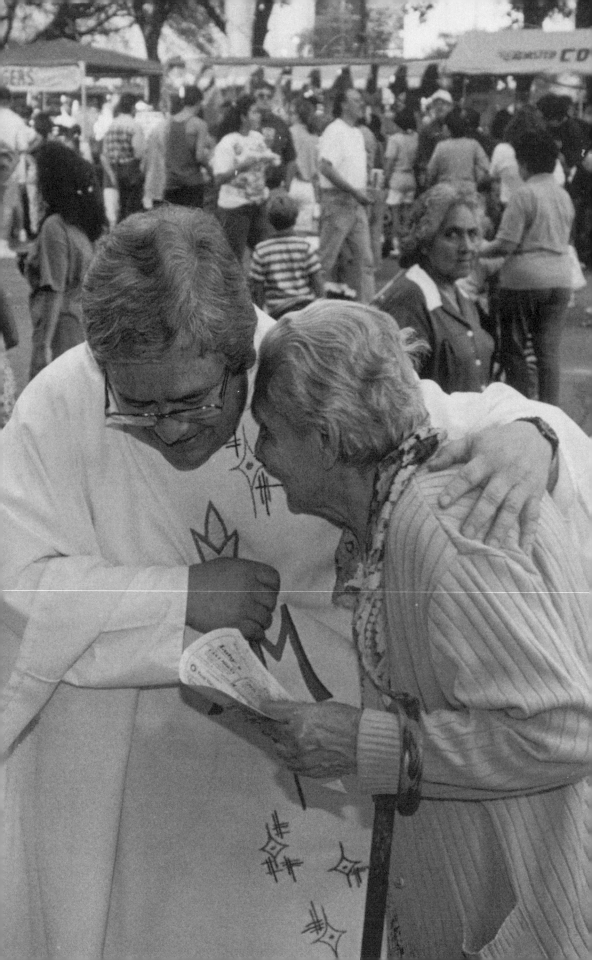

our Mexican-American reality and how to formulate creative pastoral responses to the growing needs of our people. He prefaced his invitation with the statement, "Now is the chance to prove that what you have been saying needs to be done. Let's show what our people have to offer."

I listened, consulted, and prayed, yet in the back of my mind and heart, I had accepted the archbishop's invitation the moment he mentioned it. This appointment as rector was an opportunity to dream, to motivate, and to create. Some of my close friends and colleagues had encouraged me to continue my research and writing at MACC, where I had been for the last fifteen years. They had also noted that "anyone" could serve as rector at the cathedral, which appeared to be a dying parish of elderly people.

But I saw unlimited possibilities and accepted. When I began to meet the people, I immediately fell in love with each of them. It was like coming home to a long-lost family that welcomed me with open arms. It seemed like I had known them all my life and, indeed, many of them had even carried me in their arms as a baby or scolded me when I was a young boy running around the cathedral.

Besides a homecoming, my arrival in 1983 as rector was also a rebirth. I was the first native-born San Antonian to be named rector of the cathedral. The parish was my intimate family, yet I had a new and deeper perception and appreciation of San Fernando, San Antonio, its geographical location, its history, its people, and its fascinating potential. I made a conscious decision to reclaim and recreate the religious traditions of my childhood and of my barrio as the basis for the pastoral life of the cathedral. This was not because of nostalgia but out of a conviction that these sacred traditions were not only the basis of our faith experience as Latinos and our innermost identity as a people, but that they were desperately needed for the spiritual health and salvation of the United States.

Daily for the next twelve years San Fernando was where I worked and struggled. Each day I discovered more about the incredible architectural, historical, and living treasures within its walls and surroundings. The people who come to San Fernando became my closest friends and greatest teachers. Their infused sense of reverence, ritual, and devotion is both fascinating and captivating. Today, the spiritual energy of this living mystery goes far beyond the walls of the cathedral. Through our weekly televised Mass, millions from all backgrounds and denominations throughout the Americas join together in experiencing the presence of God through our rituals and fellowship. Where does this spiritual energy come from?

As I celebrated the early pre-dawn daily Mass during any given day of the week, I felt always that we were energizing the entire city of San Antonio for one more day. As I offered the Holy Sacrifice, I felt that I was in continuity with Jesus who sacrificed himself to give us life, and with our Aztec ancestors who offered pre-dawn sacrifices to ensure that the sun would rise another day. I was in continuity with the generations from time immemorial who struggled and sacrificed to make this space of earth a more hospitable home for anyone who comes here. It was like "fueling up" the spiritual engines that give life to our city.

In the tranquillity of the daily liturgies, I felt in contact with my most ancient and even primal roots, with everyone in my city and the world, and with the generations to come until the end of time. San Fernando gave me the strength of experiencing the continuum of life. It was a mystical experience of continuity and transformation, of tradition and renewal, of death and resurrection. Never before had the words "Christ has died, Christ has risen, Christ will come again in glory" taken on such real meaning as they did during these early pre-dawn celebrations of the Holy Sacrifice.

Whether in the quiet of the early morning Mass or in the packed-like-sardines crowds of the noon Mass on Sundays or the massive faith demonstrations of Holy Week, anyone who comes to San Fernando experiences God in a very special way. As so many have told us, here God is alive and present.

As cathedrals were the unifying center of old European cities, so did San Fernando Cathedral become the unifying center, the soul, of San Antonio. My hope was that it would be a *mestizo* cathedral that would extend far beyond our own Mexican-American *mestizaje*. My goal was to unite, synthesize, and enrich various religious traditions into one coherent whole. San Fernando would become the *cathedra*, the teaching chair, from which we would learn about ourselves as the image and likeness of God and joyfully celebrate our new awareness of ourselves.

European cathedrals quickly became the centers of joyful celebrations of a redeemed humanity. This had to be a key element at San Fernando. People and clergy had to celebrate together. In the fiesta city of San Antonio, our cathedral had to be festive. We involved artists, musicians, dancers, poets, actors, vendors, festival organizers, decorators, radio, television, and the press to open up the Word of God to the masses. They all became pastoral agents of San Fernando as the cathedral strived to become a twenty-four-hour liturgical celebration of humanity.

Given the rise of secular society with its massive skyscrapers that dwarf even the greatest of cathedrals, I wondered if cathedrals could ever again play a privileged role in city and society. And my questioning went even deeper. Can the city of God exist in the very center of the cities of men and women today? Can there be a sacred space that is made sacred precisely because it violates all human barriers of division, because it dares to bring together all peoples so that they may see each other, care for one another, and work together? This must happen if we are to transform our cities from the present-day battlefields into human spaces where people can live, walk, work, and have fun in peace and harmony. We *can* learn from the past to reclaim this beautiful tradition of God as the light and center of all human activity.

EXPLORING A PEOPLE'S LIVING FAITH

In this book, we are going to explore San Fernando Cathedral, its public witness in San Antonio, the mystery of the God who is not only present, but who is easily seen, heard, smelled, touched, and tasted in and around San Fernando. Although San Fernando plays a vital role through its social, educational, and other ministries, we will look primarily at the faith of the people through their public and personal rituals, through their everyday encounters with God, and through the impact that God has beyond the walls of San Fernando.

We think it is important from the very beginning to state that this is *not* a sociological study of San Fernando, nor is it a study of any doctrine of God or of the church. Rather, it is an attempt to penetrate more deeply into the mystery of the God who lives and reigns in and with this particular community of believers. Because it studies the living faith of the people, it is a theological study, an attempt to discern the God who is alive in us and at San Fernando.

Within the church we are used to beginning with theological concepts and then implementing parish practices that conform to that theology. We are less accustomed to theologizing out of the living reality of faith as expressed by a given congregation. While we often bring in consultants to help us discern what is wrong with a congregation, we seldom study and celebrate what is good and beautiful about a believing community so that it may enrich and educate the experts. In Roman Catholicism we give a lot of theoretical importance to the *sensus fidelium*, but in actual practice we seem to operate under the conviction that the faithful are ignorant and uninformed. This attitude seems to contradict the very notion of the term "faithful." We call the people "the faithful," but do we really believe they are faithful and therefore carriers and interpreters of God's living word?

It seems that church officials and professionals are always calling the people to convert, to change, to correct, and to purify, and, at times, even to give up what is sacred to them. But is it not true that the faithful also have much to teach the church and the theological academy about the God who is alive in their lives? The poor, the simple, and the suffering have divine insight into the meaning and power of the incarnation, the cross and resurrection of Christ in our homes, streets, and neighborhoods today. The people *can* teach the church— if the church will only listen to them. This study is an attempt to do just that.

Often pastoral formation and practice seem to ignore or even deny the presence of the Spirit who is guiding and forming the Christian consciousness of the people, in this case, the Mexican Americans of San Antonio. At the San Fernando church community, however, deep respect and love for the *sensus fidelium* of the people lie at the center of parish practices. God's presence is not limited to the printed word in the sacred books or even in the sacramental presence in the tabernacle. God's presence is seen, touched, felt, smelled, heard, and tasted in the very people. This study, an attempt to know and understand the God who enters into partnership with us, begins with the truth, the goodness, and the beauty of faith as lived and expressed by the people of San Fernando, who provide us with very genuine insights into the saving truth of the gospel.

2

MEMORIES CREATE A PEOPLE

Timothy M. Matovina

Josefina has worshiped at San Fernando Cathedral for most of her eighty-five years. While she has prayed at San Fernando on many occasions, one visit to the cathedral stands out most clearly in her mind—the day her son, Alex, left for the Korean War. Like so many times before and since, on that day Josefina first prayed before the main altar and then proceeded to the side altar of Our Lady of Guadalupe, *la Virgen Morena* (the "brown Virgin"), who chose the Mexican people as her own. Josefina's gratitude for her son's safe return a few years later connects her to San Fernando as the sacred place where her plea for help was heard.

Juanita first came to San Fernando as a second-grade student in parochial school. In part because of her gratitude for the scholarships she received from the parish for both elementary and high school, she has been a member of the choir for more than six decades and served as president of the *Hijas de María* ("Daughters of Mary," an organization for young women) for some twenty-five years. She has also volunteered countless hours serving in administrative and other parish posts. She likes to pray in the morning near a Sacred Heart of Jesus image at San Fernando, an image located "away from the center of attention," which allows her to silently thank God for the education she received, the many kindnesses offered her at the parish, her health, and her home.

For Josefina, Juanita, and many other parishioners, the memories associated with San Fernando make it their spiritual home. For visitors who arrive in San Antonio, however, the full significance of the cathedral is not immediately apparent. San Antonio proclaims itself to be the site of the Alamo, that "shrine of Texas liberty" where

Mexican and Texan soldiers fought the famous battle of 1836. Photos, paintings, postcards, street signs, buildings, and businesses announce at every turn that San Antonio is proud to be the "Alamo City."

If a visitor does happen to pass by the cathedral, the building offers scant evidence that this is the historic heart of San Antonio. True, San Fernando stands in picturesque elegance between the city's two original plazas, the Plaza de las Islas and the Plaza de las Armas, and a sign near the cathedral's main doors states that it is "the oldest cathedral sanctuary in the country." But it has no classrooms, no youth center or sports facilities, no spacious grounds, no parking lot, few offices, and no large gathering place other than the church itself.

In like manner, the cathedral's interior offers little indication of San Fernando's status as the premier church in Texas. The bishop's chair is not conspicuous, nor is the altar imposing. Neither silver nor gold adorns the liturgical vessels, candlesticks, or other furnishings. No plaques or other mementos attest to the contributions of wealthy donors. The sanctuary is formed by the walls of the original adobe church built more than two hundred and fifty years ago. While the well-worn pews, stained-glass windows, ancient baptismal font, century-old pipe organ, and aged stone evoke in many newcomers a sense of awe, they do not bespeak grandeur or exalted rank. The numerous images of Jesus, Mary, and the saints reflect the majestic simplicity of a Mexican parish, not the regal splendor of a metropolitan cathedral.

For San Fernando's primarily Mexican-American congregation, however, the location and physical appearance of the cathedral illuminate its vital role in their history and contemporary life. Established by Spanish subjects more than a century before the battle of the Alamo, San Fernando is a visible sign of San Antonio's origins. Its prominent location between the city's two central plazas serves as a silent reminder of an enduring Hispanic presence and vitality. The limited facilities, humble furnishings, absence of tributes to wealthy donors, ancient sanctuary walls, rustic ambience, and familiar array of sacred images augment the congregation's sense that San Fernando is their parish church, a living testament to their heritage and spirit.

Plaques on the walls of the cathedral bear witness to the triumphs and tragedies of those who have claimed San Fernando as their spiritual home. On the one hand, recollections of events like the 1987 visit of Pope John Paul II, along with various episcopal ordinations and installations dating back over a century, clearly indicate the long-standing participation of ecclesiastical dignitaries in San Fernando's liturgical celebrations. Their participation provides official sanction for the congregation's ritual life and illuminates San Fernando's development from a frontier parish to a major urban religious center.

On the other hand, memorials to deceased parishioners recall the congregation's pain and suffering. One such memorial poetically mourns the loss of an infant, María de la Concepción Josefina Adelida. Another recounts the murder of Eugenio Navarro, who in 1838 "fell an innocent victim, by a shot from the pistol of a vindictive adversary." This "vindictive adversary" was an Anglo American named Tinsley, a newcomer to San Antonio, who reportedly was enraged by Navarro's pro-Mexican allegiance during the Texas Revolution two years earlier. Yet another reminder of hostility and death is a monument dedicated to the Alamo defenders. While this monument acclaims the courage of those who died in the Alamo battle, it also recollects one of the most violent episodes in the history of San Antonio.

The people's triumphs and tragedies are not the only elements of their collective memory recorded in San Fernando's symbolic realm. Sacred images in the cathedral unite the San Fernando faithful with heroes of faith who have long been their companions. Prominent among these companions are the community's original patrons: San Antonio, San Fernando, *Nuestra Señora de la Candelaria* (Our Lady of Candlemas), and *Nuestra Señora de Guadalupe.*

San Antonio de Padua's link to the community dates from 1691, when the first Spanish expedition arrived on this saint's feast day at the place the Native Americans called Yanaguana. The newcomers named the site in honor of San Antonio, who subsequently became the patron of the area's *presidio* and first mission. In 1731, later immigrants from the Canary Islands founded a *villa*, a town, near the *presidio*. They named the *villa* San Fernando after a relative of Spain's monarch, the future Ferdinand VI. The patronesses of the first parish church at the Villa de San Fernando were those of the Canary Islander and *mexicano* settlers in the area: *Nuestra Señora de la Candelaria* and *Nuestra Señora de Guadalupe,* respectively. The presence in

San Fernando's contemporary iconography of these original patrons connects the cathedral congregation to its ancestors and to the community's long-established celestial guardians.

The congregation's most consistent, exuberant, and long-standing public devotion is to Our Lady of Guadalupe, the patroness of the Mexican people. This devotion recalls the hope that Guadalupe brought the conquered indigenous peoples of Mexico through her 1531 apparitions to Juan Diego, an indigenous convert to Christianity. It also recalls the countless favors, blessings, and miracles that San Fernando parishioners profess their patroness has bestowed on them individually and collectively. San Fernando's Guadalupe tradition does not just recollect these past events, however, but clearly reflects the congregation's ongoing relationship with Guadalupe as a powerful guardian, intercessor, and protectress.

Nonetheless, the most prominent of San Fernando's sacred images are those of Jesus. In addition to the stations of the cross, which depict the gruesome events leading to Jesus' death, eleven other images of Jesus adorn the sanctuary and niches along the cathedral's inner walls. These images strongly emphasize the humanity of Jesus during his most vulnerable and tragic moments: as an infant, on the cross, and lying dead in the arms of his mother after the crucifixion.

In light of the violence and suffering parishioners have endured over the years, it is not surprising to find evidence of their devotion before the graphic depictions of Jesus' passion and death. The foot of Jesus on the Pietá, a statue of Mary holding the lifeless body of her son, is worn smooth from the hands of countless faithful who prayerfully touch the memory of their fallen Lord and his grieving mother. Near the main doors of the cathedral hangs *El Cristo Negro de Esquipulas* (the Black Christ of Esquipulas), a Guatemalan representation of the crucifixion. This crucifix is always surrounded by votive candles, photographs, notes, letters, braids of hair, hospital bracelets, prayers of petition and thanksgiving from devotees who identify with the rejected and condemned Galilean.

Visitors to San Fernando can easily overlook the full significance of such signs of faith, along with the historical importance of the cathedral. For parishioners like Josefina and Juanita, however, the cathedral embodies memories as specific as an answered prayer or as general and universal as a deep feeling of gratitude; the warmth of homecoming; or a sense of connectedness to past, present, and future generations. Numerous devotees who call San Fernando home find in their parish a sacred place that connects them to their brother Jesus, their mother Mary, their saint companions, and their ancestors. For them, the cathedral is a testament to their forebears and to the enduring community of faith that is their living legacy. At the same time, vivid images of their heavenly protectors and of Jesus in his moments of greatest weakness and agony remind the San Fernando congregation that persevering in faith, even through suffering and death, is the way of Jesus, the saints, and their loved ones.

Although there is no comprehensive written history of the San Fernando congregation, this history is recorded in the collective memory of the people. Even though parishioners sometimes err about specific historical facts regarding the cathedral and its faithful, they clearly articulate insights about the overall significance of San Fernando in their lives. Many parishioners defer immediately to Felipa ("Wimpie"), a parishioner whom they claim "has been at San Fernando *desde un principio*" (from the very beginning). With a wry smile, Felipa playfully responds to such claims by admitting that she may have missed a few years of the parish's 267-year history! While not literally true, these statements about Felipa's continual presence reflect the sense of ownership among San Fernando congregants. By proudly acknowledging venerable members of the community, parishioners implicitly recognize their ancestors' role in San Fernando's origins and in its ongoing flavor and spirit.

Maintaining continuity and fidelity with the past is of primary importance to the San Fernando community. The congregation celebrates this interconnectedness of past and present in rituals that bring the young children into the community, help establish their memory, and begin their journey into personhood. It is such relationships within the community that form and shape the *rostro y corazón* (the countenance and heart), which in ancient indigenous tradition indicated the character and personality of the human being. Even people who are not active church participants seek these rituals. For most Mexican Americans, all these special moments of life have a privileged place in the life of the church. It seems that this is not for purely social reasons, but in order to fulfill the deep anthropological demands of the heart that have been shaped through generations of religious practice.

The first of these rituals, baptism, is when the community claims with joy and pride a newborn as its very own and promises to nourish the child throughout the journey of life. On their next major passage into community life, the *primeras comuniones*, hundreds of young children come with their parents, grandparents, and *padrinos* (godparents) to celebrate the first time they receive the Eucharist. This entry into the community is so important that two ceremonies must be held on the same day. Cameras abound as photographs of the ritual will become part of the family's sacred icons. The photograph shows that the body of Christ is now present in the child and in the home, that the beloved child is a tabernacle of the real presence. Another important ritual in this cycle is the *quinceañera* for the young women of the parish. They come to thank God for the blessings they have received and to accept that they are now responsible for helping in the affairs of the entire community.

Sacred sites like San Fernando are vital memory places in a society frequently detached from the sense of rootedness and belonging that memory engenders. At San Fernando, memory nurtures this sense of place. Perceiving San Fernando as a symbolic center where their heritage and spirit have been passed from generation to generation, parishioners connect themselves to their ancestors and to each other by participating in the life of the San Fernando congregation and offering devotion to their community's long-standing celestial guardians.

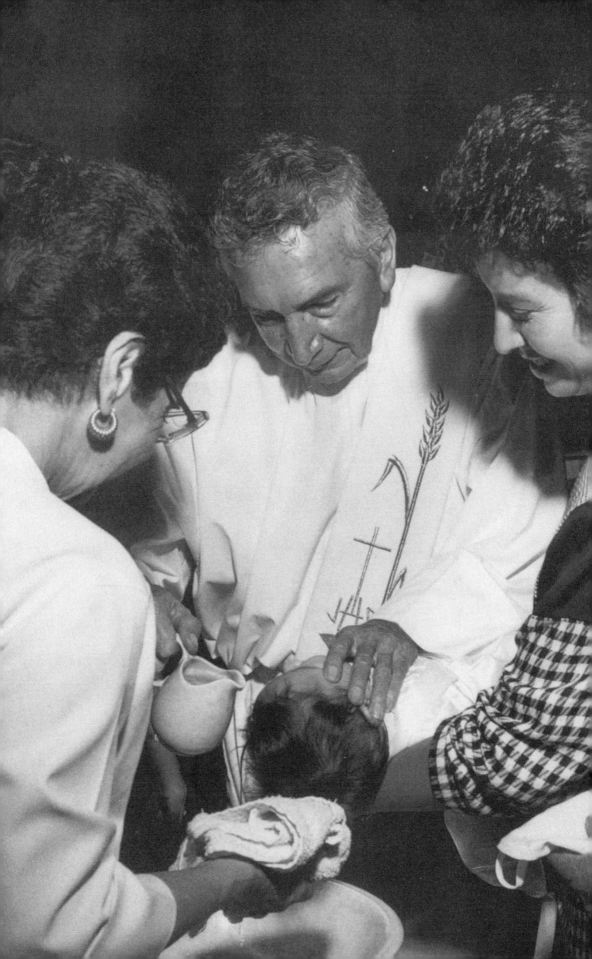

3

DEVELOPMENT OF A TRADITION

Timothy M. Matovina

San Fernando parishioners have worshiped God in the same church under the flags of Spain, Mexico, the Republic of Texas, the United States, the Confederate States of America, and then the United States again. Amidst all the changes under these successive governments, congregants celebrated the practices of their religious and cultural heritage.

FRONTIER PARISH CHURCH

The founders and early parishioners of San Fernando established a legacy of traditions to hand on to succeeding generations. The *villa* of San Fernando was founded by Spanish subjects from the Canary Islands in 1731 on a site adjacent to the *presidio* of San Antonio, established thirteen years earlier by military settlers and their families. In founding the new *villa* on the northern frontier of New Spain, the Canary Islanders formed the first self-governing town council and the first parish in Texas. At first civilians and military settlers held religious services in a makeshift house of worship; then in 1738 they began constructing a parish church that they dedicated to their patronesses *Nuestra Señora de la Candelaria* (Our Lady of Candlemas, the patroness of the Canary Islands) and *Nuestra Señora de Guadalupe*. Upon completion of the church in 1755, town council members met on December 12, the feast day of Guadalupe, and vowed before God that "now and forever we shall celebrate the feast of Blessed Mary of Guadalupe." They made similar pledges for the feasts of la Candelaria and San Fernando.

Celebration of these feast days continued throughout the eighteenth century as local residents followed the Spanish custom of honoring saints deemed to have a particular relationship with a town or village. As the first wave of military and civilian settlers interacted with one another and with later immigrants and Native Americans, however, the various cultural groups forged regional loyalties and an accompanying regional identity, an identity to which the indigenous Guadalupe had more appeal. The emergence of a "New World" *mestizo* (mixed lineage) identity and the rising popularity of the Guadalupe feast were undoubtedly enhanced by extensive intermarriage and the limited number of European-born settlers arriving in the region. As the eighteenth century progressed, December celebrations that encompassed Guadalupe Day and Christmas became the principal feasts for the local community. The lively festivities for Guadalupe and other patron feast days included religious ceremonies, social gatherings on the two plazas adjacent to the parish church, and dances held throughout the town.

Town council members, other prominent citizens, military officials, and local clergy organized ceremonies at the parish church of San Fernando (as it was popularly known) for these religious feasts and for events like the announcement of a new Spanish monarch, peace treaties, and the installation of a new town council. In 1749, for example, these leaders joined forces with the local populace to solemnize a treaty with the Apaches. They celebrated Mass in their partially completed parish church at the outset of peace talks on August 17. On August 19, soldiers, citizens, priests, and Apaches dug a hole in the center of the plaza in front of the church and placed in it the following instruments of war: a hatchet, a lance, six arrows, and a live horse! Then the various groups danced together three times around the hole; when a signal was given, they symbolized the end of hostilities by covering it.

After Mexican independence from Spain in 1821, San Fernando continued to play a prominent role in local events. The 1821 ceremony at which local residents took an oath of allegiance to Mexico included religious services at the church. Just as it had taken place under Spanish rule, the local populace then celebrated Mass at San Fernando to mark this significant moment. Mass was also celebrated on such occasions as the defeat of invading armies, the patron

Main Plaza

saint day of national leaders, the assembling of the national congress, the death of prominent political figures, and Mexican Independence Day.

Records of Independence Day—September 16, 1829—reflect San
Fernando's significance in the life of the community. The previous
evening a procession accompanied by music, church bells, and gun
salutes wound its way through the streets. On the morning of
September 16 Mass and the *Te Deum* (a religious chant of praise for
God's wondrous deeds) were offered at the church, followed in the
afternoon by another outdoor procession, a speech on the meaning of
independence, and evening dances. The next day the populace dressed
for mourning and attended a Mass offered on behalf of the dead. Until
the beginning of the Texas Revolution (1835-1836), San Antonians
continued their long-standing practice of inviting elected and military
officials to cooperate with local clergy to organize civic and religious
celebrations at San Fernando and its surrounding plazas.

By the time the Republic of Texas won independence from Mexico
in 1836, the December celebration that encompassed Guadalupe Day
and Christmas had already been the principal religious feast in San
Antonio for decades. The town council planned the December festivities, known as *la temporada de fiestas* (the season of feasts), which
spilled out into the plaza in front of San Fernando. Various forms of
entertainment complemented the religious rites observed by the
parish community.

A CENTER FOR MEXICAN RITUALS

After the political separation of Texas from the Mexican Republic,
the church of San Fernando remained the focal point for Mexican
religious and cultural traditions in San Antonio, despite the shifting
historical context and rapid demographic change. The number of
Anglo-American and European (especially German) immigrants increased significantly in San Antonio after Texas independence in 1836
and grew even more rapidly after the United States annexed Texas in
1845. In 1850, Hispanic residents numbered less than half of San
Antonio's population for the first time in the settlement's history.
Twenty-five years later, residents of Mexican descent comprised less

than one-fourth of the city's population; both Germans and Anglo Americans had eclipsed them in number. However, immigration from south of the border increased during the rule of Mexican president Porfirio Díaz (1876-1880, 1884-1911) and accelerated even more after the outbreak of the Mexican Revolution in 1910. This influx of newcomers augmented San Antonio's Mexican-descended population significantly; by 1970 that population comprised more than half of city residents for the first time in 120 years.

Not surprisingly, the political influence of Mexican residents diminished as the city's demographic profile shifted during the 1800s. In 1842 Mayor Juan N. Seguín was run out of town by enemies he described as "straggling American adventurers" who threatened and murdered Mexican families in order to steal their land. No other Mexican-descended citizen served as mayor until the election of Henry Cisneros nearly one hundred forty years later. When Texas became a state, Mexican San Antonians lost control of the city council their ancestors had established and led for more than a century. During the following century they held less than 5 percent of the city council posts, and they have never regained a majority on the city council.

After Texas statehood, citizens of Mexican heritage increasingly became a working underclass and lost most of their land holdings. Despite numerous signs of modernization and economic development, such as the city's first railroad lines, electric street lights, telephone exchange, chartered banks, and streetcars, this downward socioeconomic movement continued through the closing decades of the nineteenth century. Twentieth-century Mexican immigrants to San Antonio included a few wealthy families, and a nascent middle class of Mexican citizens emerged during the 1920s. By 1930, however, almost 90 percent of Mexican-descended residents were in the city's poorest economic class.

The diminishing influence of residents of Mexican descent was also reflected in the use of Spanish for public affairs in San Antonio. City council minutes, which had been recorded in Spanish for more than a century, were kept in both Spanish and English from 1838 to 1844, and thereafter exclusively in English. In 1858, local elected officials instituted a program of teacher certification for the public

schools and decreed that public funds would be available for the salaries of certified teachers solely in schools where the principal language was English. By the 1920s Anglo-American students formed SSS (Stop Speaking Spanish) clubs at public schools to ensure that the official ban on the use of Spanish was enforced.

The parish of San Fernando was not immune to change during this turbulent period. In 1840, Pope Gregory XVI appointed Vincentian priest Jean Marie Odin as the area's first vice prefect apostolic. Shortly after his arrival in Texas, Odin visited San Antonio and removed the city's two native-born priests, Refugio de la Garza and José Antonio Valdéz, claiming that their ministry was ineffective and that they had broken their priestly vows by having wives and children. He replaced the native clergy with his Spanish confrere Miguel Calvo. San Fernando would not have another pastor of Mexican heritage until the appointment of Virgilio Elizondo in 1983. Most clergy assigned to San Fernando during the last half of the nineteenth century were French. Then in 1902 Spanish priests and brothers of the Missionary Sons of the Immaculate Heart of Mary, known as Claretians, began their seventy-six-year tenure at the cathedral. While contemporary parishioners recall the dedication of the Claretians, they also recall that, unlike Virgilio Elizondo and other Mexican-descended clergy, the Spanish priests were stern and often overbearing.

Despite the absence of native-born clergy, San Fernando remained the one institution in San Antonio that retained a Mexican flavor. During the mid-nineteenth century, Father Calvo and the other European clergy who succeeded him consistently used Spanish in their ministries and participated in the congregation's long-standing religious and cultural traditions. Accompanied by the new clergy, San Fernando parishioners organized public rituals and festivities for Our Lady of Guadalupe, Christmas, San Fernando, San Antonio, San Juan, San Pedro, and other feasts. Most conspicuous among these rites was the annual Guadalupe feast, which the parish community celebrated in the Mexican style, with a colorful procession, flowers, candles, elaborate decorations adorning the Guadalupe image and their parish church, gun and cannon salutes, extended ringing of the church bells, and large crowds at services conducted in Spanish.

Given the declining political and economic influence of Mexican residents, the use of English in local government and public schools, and the loss of San Fernando's native clergy, these feast-day celebrations provided an ongoing means of communal expression uniting parishioners and linking them to their ancestral heritage. Flowing from San Fernando into the city's plazas and streets, celebrations like those for Our Lady of Guadalupe were a public manifestation of the congregation's persistent allegiance to the Mexican Catholic traditions received from their forebears.

These public celebrations clearly illuminate San Fernando's role as a vital center for the congregation's treasured cultural expressions of faith. Perhaps fear and anger at their economic and political displacement intensified congregants' religious devotion and commitment to their parish center. The symbolic meaning of this parish center was noted in 1854 by one visitor to the city:

> Around the plaza are American hotels, and new glass-fronted stores, alternating with sturdy battlemented Spanish walls, and confronted by the dirty, grim, old stuccoed stone cathedral, whose cracked bell is now clunking for vespers, in a tone that bids us no welcome, as more of the intruding race who have caused all this progress, on which its traditions, like its imperturbable dome, frown down.

For the San Fernando congregation, their parish was the only institution that had not been taken over by Anglo-American or other immigrants to their city. As their sole surviving institution, San Fernando was both a reminder of San Antonio's origins under the government of New Spain and a ritual center where parishioners celebrated their communal identity.

After the Civil War, Catholic leaders renovated and enlarged San Fernando, and in 1874 it was declared a cathedral by Pope Pius IX. With its new status San Fernando hosted the installation and consecration of bishops, the celebration of a papal jubilee, and the visits of ecclesiastical dignitaries like Cardinal James Gibbons of Baltimore, and Archbishop Francis Satolli, the pope's first apostolic delegate to the United States.

As diocesan liturgical celebrations multiplied at San Fernando, the observance of Mexican feasts in some ways diminished. According to one newspaper report, Bishop Anthony Dominic Pellicer, the first bishop of the new San Antonio diocese (1874-1880), prohibited the traditional Christmas Eve celebration of midnight Mass with adoration of the Holy Child "because of the intrusion of improper and disorderly persons with the vast throngs of all classes, races, and religions, who poured into the cathedral" on that occasion. Another newspaper report stated that an elderly San Antonio resident, identified as Don Pablo, bemoaned the decline of the annual feasts previously celebrated with great splendor at San Fernando. On the feast of Our Lady of Guadalupe in 1878, yet another report recounted the public displays of Guadalupan devotion in former days, but added that these displays had died out.

Nonetheless, newcomers and visitors to San Antonio noted that San Fernando still retained a pronounced Mexican flavor even after the parish church became a cathedral. One observer wrote that many descendants of the original parishioners worshiped at the new cathedral, while another described San Fernando as "an old, venerable Spanish cathedral, where dark-brown penitents kneel on cold stones, saying their beads." Yet another stated bluntly that "San Fernando Cathedral is Mexican Catholic."

The perception of San Fernando as a Mexican cathedral was undoubtedly reinforced by ongoing parish traditions and feasts. To be sure, public rituals for Our Lady of Guadalupe and other feasts were not as conspicuous as those of previous eras; there is no evidence that they spilled onto the plazas and streets with devotional practices like gun salutes, cannonading, and outdoor processions. But church services and other feast-day festivities continued. Moreover, despite some diminishment of Mexican rites at San Fernando, its new status as a cathedral gave official sanction to the ongoing observance of established feasts like those of the congregation's Guadalupan patroness. Such ongoing traditions as the annual Guadalupe rites, which had thrived at San Fernando for well over a century, linked parishioners with their forebears and enabled a distinctively Mexican Catholic religious and cultural ethos to survive in San Antonio.

During the first decades of the twentieth century, an influx of Mexican exiles increased the San Fernando congregation fivefold to some twenty thousand worshipers. Included among the exiles were numerous Mexican prelates, clergy, and women religious, particularly during the Mexican Revolution and after Mexican president Plutarco Elías Calles (1924-1928) enforced anticlerical articles in the Mexican Constitution of 1917. Although not formally assigned to the cathedral, many of these bishops, priests, and sisters assisted San Fernando's Spanish Claretian clergy and animated the community's devotional and ritual life. In 1926, Pope Pius XI established the archdiocese and province of San Antonio. San Fernando then became a metropolitan cathedral, adding further prominence to this center of Spanish-speaking Catholicism.

With the support of the Spanish Claretians and the exiled Mexican clergy and women religious, the growing San Fernando congregation revivified San Fernando's tradition of public ritual. By early 1930, San Fernando parishioners led processions through the plazas and streets for celebrations like *Cristo Rey* (Christ the King), Our Lady of Guadalupe, the *posadas* (when the pilgrims Mary and Joseph seek lodging in Bethlehem), and for the entrance rite of the First Communion Mass. The revived Guadalupe processions were held on two nights: the procession of roses on December 11 (to commemorate the roses that the indigenous neophyte Juan Diego gathered as a sign from Guadalupe), and the procession of lights on December 12. During the 1950s and early 1960s, members of other parishes processed to San Fernando to join the cathedral congregation for the Guadalupe feast. During this period, as many as forty thousand faithful from more than one hundred parishes converged on San Fernando for an outdoor Mass in honor of their patroness.

This resurgence of public ritual was primarily due to the participation of exiled Mexicans at San Fernando. Indeed, it is striking that the reanimation of religious processions through the city streets and plazas occurred during the suppression of the Mexican church under President Calles, an era when numerous exiled bishops, priests, women religious, and lay Catholics joined the San Fernando congregation. Significantly, in the procession of lights for Our Lady of Guadalupe, participants bore torches decorated with the colors of the Mexican flag, while members of the various parish societies

marched under their respective banners and Mexican flags. This juxtaposition of religious and national symbols reflects a sentiment articulated in San Antonio's *La Prensa* newspaper during this period: "The day that the cult of the Indian Virgin [of Guadalupe] disappears, the Mexican nationality will also disappear." Clearly, Mexican exiles demonstrated their national allegiance through such Mexican Catholic devotions.

At the same time, however, the newly arrived Mexican exiles did not establish a new faith community at San Fernando; rather, they enhanced a faith community that had been functioning for almost two centuries. While some religious and cultural traditions had weakened, particularly when San Antonio's Mexican residents were numerically overwhelmed during the latter decades of the 1800s, surviving feasts like that of Our Lady of Guadalupe presented the immigrant newcomers with familiar symbols and rituals that united them with San Fernando congregants. Together they found in the cathedral a sacred place where they could remember and celebrate devotional traditions rooted in their religious and cultural heritage.

Throughout the long history of the San Fernando congregation, the memory and celebration of Mexican Catholic traditions united parishioners and created a sense of common identity and peoplehood. As these traditions passed from generation to generation, devotional practices such as public processions, the use of flowers and banners, the adornment of sacred images, gun salutes, and cannonading were altered, added, or abandoned. While the prominence of some feasts has fluctuated over the years, at times declining and at other times increasing, annual rites in honor of Our Lady of Guadalupe have remained the most popular celebrations since the parish's beginnings. Over time, though, other feasts like Christ the King have been added as the San Fernando ritual tradition continues to evolve.

Like their predecessors, contemporary congregants perceive the cathedral as a sacred place that preserves their ancient rites and heritage. The collective memory of today's congregants emphasizes the continuity of sacred traditions celebrated at the cathedral. After a recent Good Friday passion drama in which thousands accompanied Jesus carrying his cross through San Antonio's downtown streets, a parishioner stated, "Every step down the Via Dolorosa is an affirmation of our past, an understanding of our present, and a courageous entrance into our future. Every year, as the procession winds its way from the Market Square to the cathedral, our community deepens its roots." This rootedness in a common past, now nearly three centuries in the making, is clearly a powerful force for creating a sense of common identity and peoplehood.

SAN FERNANDO TODAY

Under the pastoral leadership of Virgilio Elizondo, the San Antonio-born rector of San Fernando from 1983 through 1995, San Fernando's rich tradition of public ritual and imagery was revivified and further developed. Elizondo's pastoral vision was based on the insight that although his people had been externally conquered and oppressed, they had never been crushed or dominated. Along with other indigenous peoples in the territories that became New Spain (and later Mexico), they were first conquered by the Spaniards and then later by the United States. The effects of this second conquest continue, putting pressures on Mexican Americans to assimilate, to abandon Mexican ways for the American way. Despite this pressure, Elizondo perceives in his people a *mestizo* identity, one that is neither Mexican nor Anglo American, neither Spanish nor indigenous, but a dynamic mixture of these root cultures. He enjoins his fellow *mestizos* not to identify themselves in a negative way as "not Mexican" or "not American," but to claim the positive identity of *mestizos* who have the advantage of knowing two (or more) cultures. This *mestizo* identity entails both a calling and mission. It is those people who know multiple cultures and who have borne the pain of conquest and rejection who can lead the way to build a society in which the divisive barriers between peoples are broken, particularly the false belief that God blesses one people in their quest to conquer another.

Elizondo enabled his people to embrace their *mestizo* identity and mission by celebrating with them the imagery of a *mestizo* God, a God who is open to all peoples and their traditions. He proclaims the *mestizo* origins of Jesus as a Galilean, a borderland reject caught between the Roman occupation force in Palestine and the Jewish temple elite, who claimed Galileans were "impure." Yet it is the *mestizo* Galilean, caught between two cultures, who rejects rejection and

the destructive barriers that separate peoples. Similarly, Elizondo
states that Guadalupe "is neither an Indian goddess nor a European
Madonna; she is something new. She is neither Spanish nor Indian
and yet she is both and more.... She is the first truly American person
and as such the mother of the new generations to come." Thus she
provides hope and inspiration for a *mestizo* people called to create a
new future and a new humanity.

As San Fernando's rector, Elizondo celebrated the God imagery of
the San Fernando congregation through his preaching, teaching, and
pastoral leadership, but most especially through his considerable
efforts to affirm and enrich the people's traditions of public ritual.
His openness to other peoples and religious traditions paved the way
for numerous other devotees to join with the worshiping community at the cathedral. While Mexican-descended congregants remain
the parish's mainstay, today San Fernando is a spiritual home for an
incredibly diverse assemblage of peoples.

Under the guidance of Father Elizondo, the development of an
internationally televised Sunday Mass has attracted a weekly congregation of nearly ten million people—from various religious, cultural,
and socioeconomic backgrounds—who worship at the cathedral via
television. Similarly, long-standing traditions like the celebrations in
honor of Our Lady of Guadalupe increasingly encompass both established parishioners and other devotees, who celebrate their treasured
Mexican Catholic expressions of faith. New rites like the city-wide
Thanksgiving service and the annual Pilgrimage of Hope for those
afflicted with HIV/AIDS gather Hindus, Buddhists, Muslims, Jews,
and Christians from various denominations for interfaith services
at the cathedral. As one San Antonio reporter wrote in 1986, contemporary San Fernando is the "celestial center of San Antonio," a
sanctuary of the spirit embraced by a vast array of city residents
and visitors.

The growing number of interfaith worship services and the liturgical participation of people from diverse cultures and creeds attest
to the San Fernando congregation's openness to religious traditions
other than their own. Like others who attend interfaith services at the
cathedral, San Fernando parishioners respond fervently to ritual practices like Buddhist chants and Christian hymns, Native American

dance and Mexican mariachi music, the proclamation of the Muslim Koran and the Hebrew scriptures. While the San Fernando community is true to its own Mexican Catholic traditions and God imagery, parishioners welcome diverse faith expressions as an enrichment of that heritage, creating a sacred environment in which the fragmented children of God unite in common fellowship and worship.

4

ICONS OF THE SACRED

Virgilio P. Elizondo

"The building is not the focus, but the people. Anyone can feel just as comfortable in a silk tie and dark suit, in work clothes or anything else. Here we all participate as equals in the same way—nowhere else but at San Fernando Cathedral."

San Fernando is a beautiful cathedral, but its treasure is greater and more beautiful and dynamic than just its building, even filled as it is with history and memories. The uniqueness of San Fernando is precisely its people in their physical presence, traditions, everyday lives, devotions, prayers, and rituals. Everything about them comes together to present the living and life-giving mystery of San Fernando, which is nothing less than the mystery of the living God in the center of a city. So the story of San Fernando is the story of the revelation of the mystery of God's presence in this particular location—God's Word made flesh.

Some of the people of San Fernando are descendants of the original settlers—not the *conquistadores* who came to conquer, but the simple, hard-working immigrants who created a new city. They arrived in San Antonio with no illusions of gold or a fountain of youth. Only through hard work and cooperation with the local inhabitants would they build a community of free citizens. From the beginning, whether by choice or necessity, they intermingled with the native people and the Mexicans who were already in San Antonio to form the beginnings of what would eventually become San Fernando's and San Antonio's deepest identity and most obvious characteristic: hospitality growing from a multi-ethnic identity that

43

joins together people of all social classes. Today, these hard-working and hospitable people form the mainstay of the cathedral's parishioners. They continue to welcome everyone: from the poorest to the wealthiest, from the well-dressed to the shabby, from descendants of the original settlers to newly arrived undocumented immigrants. No one is left standing outside the door.

One of the greatest gifts of the people of San Fernando is their acceptance and love of life, whether in success or in failure, in poverty or in abundance, in good times or in tragedy, in their homes or in homelessness. Despite obstacles, contradictions, and hardships, their affirmation and love of life witness powerfully to the unquestioned depth of their faith and hope. These people have never lost their sense of beauty, dignity, and self-worth, both as individuals and as a community. Their lived faith in a tender and compassionate God has a simplicity that, while it may shock some, inspires others. Their God is much more a God of people than of church buildings, doctrines, rules, convents, or monasteries. Their God is experienced, touched, seen, and heard.

Some time ago, I was standing in front of the cathedral waiting for a society wedding, which was running late. A parishioner named Teresita, a heavily rouged "bag lady" who lives under one of the bridges and keeps all her belongings in a grocery cart, started visiting with me about the latest developments in the downtown area. She enjoys being in and around the cathedral and visits readily with anyone and everyone. While she owns nothing but what she carries with her, she has no lack of self-confidence or human dignity, and she converses about San Antonio as if she were the mayor or the head of the chamber of commerce. Her one complaint is the lack of public bathrooms in the downtown area—not for herself, but for the poor tourists.

As the wedding party arrived in a procession of white stretch limousines, Teresita observed, "I like to see these people come to our church." There was no doubt in her sense of belonging and ownership, neither was there any sense of resentment about the rich coming to the house of the poor. Although she didn't elaborate, behind her statement seemed to be the conviction that everyone is welcome in the Father's household—the Mother always welcomes all her children.

When the elegant mother of the bride, weighed down with heavy jewelry and covered with furs (somewhat ridiculous given the near summer heat of San Antonio's winter), descended from the limousine, Teresita immediately recognized Rosie, an old girlfriend from her neighborhood. She rushed over and greeted her old school friend with great enthusiasm. It was immediately evident that the enthusiasm was not mutual. The mother of the bride appeared to be politely trying to get rid of her as Teresita was joyfully recalling the fun of their school days. Teresita caught the hint. As she waved goodbye to Rosie, she said with great pride and sincerity, "I am so honored that you chose my church for the wedding of your daughter."

As I walked back to the sacristy to vest for the wedding, I reflected on what I had just seen and heard. Would Rosie have welcomed Teresita to her church? Teresita and many like her are the reality and the glory of San Fernando. They are the true property owners of God's household; they always welcome anyone and everyone. Together, they are the merciful father of the Prodigal Son, except here the parent welcomes not only one returning child, but all children without exception. Teresita's unprepared and spontaneous witness in front of the church was much more realistic and powerful than any sermon I could preach on the universality of God's love and welcome. This is seeing the loving face of God and hearing God's merciful voice calling an unconditional welcome to all.

In the past Tejanos or Mexicanos were often denied entrance to many of the institutions of a city, state, and nation, including Catholic churches. San Fernando has always been a parish home where Tejanos or Mexicanos have never had to explain to anyone who they are, why they are the way they are, or why they worship the way they do. The first thing that is immediately obvious to anyone who enters San Fernando is that it is the home of Mexican and Latino immigrants, many of whom have just arrived and are scared to be anywhere else. For a long time the cathedral's leadership had great difficulty with patrols of the Immigration and Naturalization Service (INS) who would circle the cathedral picking up suspects as they left the church. An official protest was launched when an INS vehicle violated the ancient right of sanctuary by entering the cathedral space to apprehend some suspected "illegals." Indignation was both holy and righteous at this persecution of poor migrants by the INS patrols who took advantage of the faith of the people.

San Fernando is also the home of all the Latino poor who do not feel at home anywhere else, including a large group of Tejanos, descendants of the original *mestizos* of the area, who have been working hard for generations to make a home their children will be proud of. Although other backgrounds—social, cultural, and racial—are also represented, it is primarily through the perseverance and hard work of these Tejanos and arriving immigrants from Mexico that San Fernando has continued to evolve and develop, has maintained its religious traditions, and has defied the commonly accepted notion that Mexicans cannot sustain a parish.

The composite face and body of San Antonio with its rich variety of peoples is easily visible on any ordinary day at San Fernando. The people who enter the cathedral are workers, bankers, teachers, administrators, shopkeepers, professionals, maids, gardeners, janitors, judges, undocumented "aliens," elected officials, waiters, security guards, day workers, welfare recipients, street people, winos, prostitutes, and, of course, tourists and pilgrims.

Many of the people live on below-average incomes in public housing, in senior-citizen homes, in crowded one-room apartments. Most homes have many children, some belonging to the families and others dropped there by parents who for one reason or another could not keep them. Hardly any of the children have braces because their families cannot afford dental work. Many people are overweight, not because they overeat but because they cannot afford proper nutritious foods or exercise gyms. Although wardrobes are very basic, the people are always neat and proper. Even the poorest are not without dignity.

Richard, a disabled and unemployed man who lives alone on a very minimal income, is the head sacristan. No canon of St. Peter's in Rome or elsewhere could carry out his job with greater dignity. Ramona, a part-time hairdresser and domestic, presides over the daily liturgies along with the celebrant and leads the congregation in song. Felipa "Wimpie," a retired factory worker who takes over the management of the parish on weekends, is, in fact, the informal "permanent rector" of San Fernando. Alfredo, a handsome and gifted singer

who, with proper management, could easily have been a TV star, has chosen to work around the cathedral in any way he can. Felix and David are retired men who love to spend time at the cathedral making themselves useful. Josefina's life mission is to decorate the altar of Our Lady of Guadalupe and to collect money for the children's summer school. Maggie, a local store clerk, is always ready to help anyone who needs help. The list could go on indefinitely: Janie, Vangie, Dulce, Manuel, Mario, Philip, Henry, Charles, and many others.

There are also professionals who have found a new life in San Fernando. Our choir was directed for many years by Mary Esther, who created one of the most efficient multicultural arts programs in the country for the San Antonio Independent School District. Her husband Joe, our first Mexican-American state senator, directs the *Dia de los Muertos* celebration. Lucille is our first Mexican-American woman to earn a Ph.D. and obtain a major position in the San Antonio Independent School District. Joe Nick is associate superintendent of public schools in San Antonio. Victor is executive director of NAFTA's Inter-American Bank. Lionel founded a major advertising agency that serves all of Spanish-speaking America. Al is currently president of that agency and a business and community leader in his own right. Pat, an outstanding lawyer, was recently written up in the *Wall Street Journal*. Kathy owns and operates a successful public relations/advertising firm. Rosemary has the most successful catering firm in San Antonio.

But there is still another group that feels equally at home. Robert is a young man who cannot tolerate liquor and gets drunk with one sip of beer. He spends much time at the church, especially during funerals. Gloria, who died a couple of years ago, was a three-hundred-pound woman with the mentality of an eight-year-old who just liked being in the church. Marty was a master at bending his leg so that it looked like half of it was missing, an effective trick for a beggar. When he thought no one was watching, he would shoulder his crutch and walk away. Margarita, an elderly lady, sat in the first pew and hit with her cane anyone who appeared to want her seat. There was also the man who, at communion, simply took the host and walked away with it. I followed him to ask what he was going to do with it. With great pride, he opened a leather folder and showed me where he was going to place it. He had a collection of hosts from other churches but lacked one from San Fernando. He said he loved Jesus and wanted to have as much of Jesus as possible.

Visitors to San Fernando often note the genuineness of the people and of the community, which is both appealing and liberating. This is an assembly of people just as they are, bound together in a mystical solidarity that overcomes the barriers that would normally separate these very same people anywhere else.

In other parts of San Antonio, or the world, many San Fernando parishioners might appear as the unnoticed, the unwelcome, the undesirables. Yet at San Fernando, each is important, and each contributes in a special way to the community. Their dignity and self-composure, their pride in their children, their ease of movement around the church all attest to their firm conviction that they are at home. At San Fernando the poor are never merely tolerated or apologetically hidden; instead, they are the principal hosts of the household. The assurance with which the ushers welcome everyone, the pride of altar servers, lectors, and communion ministers, the enthusiasm of the choirs all proclaim that we are all God's children with the dignity, security, and joy of being together in God's household.

Indeed, the gospel comes alive in the personal stories of San Fernando's members: being underpaid at work; humiliated by their bosses; abandoned by their spouses; ignored by their children in their old age; manipulated and tricked out of their homes by some quick-talking salesperson; jailed for some insignificant happening; unable to afford food, medicine, electricity, or water; heartbroken because they don't know how to tell their parents they are gay or infected with AIDS. Their resilience and their struggles of daily life are those of the people drawn to Jesus, because in him and with him they find the humanity denied them by the ordinary world. They are not bitter, only grateful for the magnificence of God—the insights and assurance of their faith. They may include unwed pregnant mothers, poor parents about to give birth to a child, or immigrants with young children who are fleeing the atrocities of their countries.

The composite body and face of San Fernando is like that of the Risen Lord, who in his glorious state still exhibited the wounds of the crucifixion. San Fernando is a gathering of suffering and struggling people who have never allowed the pains and tears of life to rob them of the joy of living, nor have they relinquished their pride or dignity because of the multiple insults and injuries of society. The wounds are still there in the bodies, minds, and hearts of the people, but they are without doubt a glorious, resurrected people of great joy, simplicity, and enthusiasm.

In the joyful and respectful acceptance of one another, the people who come to San Fernando become the living bread that gives life to the world. One parishioner said, "I like to come to San Fernando because here people sense the goodness of their God. Every congregation has its character and San Fernando's is a radical openness to people of all walks of life and traditions. Here we experience God's acceptance of all people. Yes, the ability to transcend divisions between people gives San Fernando its beautifully unique character."

San Fernando is truly a community of the beatitudes. Those who are poor because they own little or nothing in this world are happy in the knowledge and security that they are property owners in God's kingdom. Those who are hungry because of their lack in this world are filled with the joy of living in God's presence. Those who weep because of the disasters and failures of this life can laugh together in the realization that all the sufferings of this world are as nothing for those who put their trust in God. Others in society might ridicule and reject many of our people, but we rejoice together, we sing and dance, we laugh and play, we pray and worship because within San Fernando we are already in the presence of God.

The disciples of Jesus are clearly present in the men and women who minister in the parish through singing, assisting with the liturgy, welcoming people, and maintaining the parish building. While the names of the persons might differ, the characters are the same. Jesus is as accessible in San Fernando as he was in Galilee or Jerusalem, moving through the crowds, lingering to talk with a questioning man, stopping to comfort a sorrowing woman, offering grace and encouragement for a people who seek to persevere in the way of faith.

5

CONVERSATIONS WITH GOD

Virgilio P. Elizondo

People come to San Fernando to touch and be touched by God physically and spiritually. For them God is not a distant deity, but a very real bodily presence with a face, clothing, size, smell, voice, and social position. Their God is one who knows them and their *mestizo* experience. On any given day, at any time of the day or night, people are in deep personal conversation with God, Jesus, and the saints, their closest friends. Their devotion to the *Cristo Negro de Esquipulas* (Black Christ from Guatemala), the tabernacle, the *Santo Niño* (the Holy Child), the *Sagrado Corazón* (the Sacred Heart) witness, with no doubt whatsoever, to their understanding of a personal presence and a willingness to listen. Just as in the time of the Galilean Jesus, when people did not hesitate to speak out, touch, or ask for favors, so it is today. The faithful leave personal notes, gifts, photos of loved ones, flowers wrapped in newspaper.

In the late 1960s and the '70s, when the liturgical reforms of Vatican II were first being implemented, many clergy (including clergy at San Fernando) were set on making churches "Christocentric" by removing statues that supposedly diverted attention from Christ. One of the *viejitas* (elderly ladies) of San Fernando objected. A custodian of the church building and of our sacred tradition, someone who "intuitively knows when the gospel is being served or destroyed" (*Catechism of the Catholic Church*, 1676), she was not about to be confused by theoretical ideas. When the clergy explained why it was proper to remove the statues of the saints from around the church so that Christ would be the visible center of all church life, she very politely and with great confidence presented another point of view: "In the gospel stories, Jesus always appeared as a people lover. He was always surrounded by his friends, and even his enemies. Why do you now want to strip him of his friends who are also our friends? Yes, Christ should be in the center but not by himself alone, stripped of all his friends. Christ should appear as he appeared in the gospel stories, surrounded by people of all kinds, friends and enemies, saints and sinners alike, but never the center of an empty space."

And she was correct. Without knowing the people around Jesus—what they were saying, doing, and thinking—and conversing with them, we cannot really know Jesus. The early Christians realized very quickly that it was in his relationships with people that the fullness of Christ would shine forth. This is how they moved from the early proclamations of the death and resurrection of Jesus to develop a memory of the entire Jesus event. The gospel stories, with people's observations, questions, doubts, petitions, and even criticisms and condemnations, became essential parts of the revelation of the total mystery of Jesus of Nazareth.

The *Cristo Negro de Esquipulas* is one of the living mysteries of San Fernando. Parishioners know very little about this representation of Christ and ask few questions, but their devotion to its miraculous powers continues to grow and spread among Catholics and Protestants alike. Throughout the day, people come in to offer candles, flowers, notes, pictures, or simply to be there. Right next to the *Cristo Negro* is the *Madre Dolorosa* (the Sorrowful Mother) with the body of her dead son on her lap. Often during the day men and women, young and old, tenderly touch or hold the feet of the figure of Mary. They seem to say, "No one out there understands what is happening to me, but you do! You alone understood what was happening to your crucified son. You alone can understand and appreciate what I am going through."

San Martín de Porres, the mulatto saint from Peru, is also present. A healer of animals and humans alike during his life, he continues to be a healer today for the *mestizo* people who recognize him as "one of ours." His life was marked by simplicity. Rejected because of his mulatto status, he dedicated his life to the loving and healing service of everyone, demonstrating the falsity of any society that builds some up by putting others down.

Other popular images of saints include St. Anthony, St. Francis, St. Jude, and St. Joseph, who stand as companions to *Nuestra Señora de*

San Juan de los Lagos (Our Lady of St. John of the Lakes) and *Nuestra Señora de Guadalupe* (Our Lady of Guadalupe). Images of Mary and devotions to Our Lady at San Fernando and throughout the Latin American world are expressions not only of Mary of the gospels, but also of the feminine and maternal aspects of God. Guadalupe, for example, is not only associated with the Mother of God, but she is also the historical mother of the Mexican people and of the people of the Americas. As one woman parishioner said, "The church is so complicated, but she is so simple! She understands us."

But, at the center of all the devotions, and the immediate focus upon entering the cathedral, is the crucifix. Upon entering the church, it is as if the choir is singing, "Christ is dead, Christ is risen, Christ is alive and present for you." No matter where they stop to pray, most people end up before the crucifix with the tabernacle at its feet. They remain in the utter silence of being consciously in the presence of God. No one has to explain it to them, they simply know it.

Occasionally, a young Japanese man stands as if in a trance at the foot of the cross by the Blessed Sacrament altar. Neither a Catholic nor a Christian, he is a university student in San Antonio who likes to be there because he feels deep peace and a sense of communion with the cosmos. He has said, "Here I experience what I think you Christians call God." Stranger and parishioner alike see and know the divine presence. Here they experience their own ultimate existence, their personal encounter with the holiness of God, just by being who they are.

God's transcendence is attested to by the great number of candles throughout the cathedral. There are no electric candles in this ancient shrine which connects the present with both the past and the future, and the earthly with the heavenly. On the special feast days of Holy Thursday, Good Friday, and All Souls' Day, the numbers of burning candles multiply. The candle is a form of petition, friendship, adoration, and thanksgiving, a simple but profound confession of faith in the all-embracing power of divine providence.

Regular parishioners are comfortable with their closeness to God. In the words of one worshiper, "Here we can be who we are without having to apologize or explain to anyone else why we Mexicans like to do things our way." They dress as they choose, in silk suits or working clothes, and they are never out of place. They pray as they want, where they want. They bring their babies with them, and no one bothers them if a baby cries. They light their candles, and no one will take them away.

At San Fernando, the basis of all devotions and gestures is a deep sense of the personal relationship with God and all of God's family. Even though people of all races, religions, and social status are present, it is obvious that it is the brown-skinned *mestizo* poor—whether Tejanos, Mexican, Mexican American, or Central American—that own San Fernando and make it their home. Faces are wrinkled by constant exposure to the wind and sun of outdoor labor, bodies are often overweight due to lack of proper nutrition, dress is simple due to poverty, children are many because of the people's love of life. Young, middle-aged, old, they struggle through life and find fellowship with the saints and others around the church. Few are sad or depressed, for this is the festive home of the *mestizo* God of San Antonio.

TALKING WITH GOD

The voice of any people is heard and recognized through its language. Language, which represents a people's innermost identity, includes not just the formal language learned in schools, but even more strikingly the everyday language of ordinary folks, the common expressions, proverbs, and analogies of feeling: love, hate, ridicule, joy, surprise, disgust. Language also comprises the gestures—the hand-shake, eye contact or lack of it, an invitation to sit, a kiss. Such body language often communicates even more effectively than verbal language. This is true of the community of San Fernando, whose verbal and nonverbal language tells of the people's relationship with God and expresses their theology.

The Voice of Silence

Each day the ancient bells of San Fernando ring out through the city, and the majestic sounds of the pipe organ spill out into the surrounding plazas. Yet, for most San Fernando worshipers the most beautiful voice heard is the voice of the silence of God. This is not the silence of an absent or distant God, but the active, inviting silence of God listening attentively to all the children of the family. The message of

the silence says, "Speak your heart for I am a listening and compassionate God. You have nothing to fear, for I am here only for you."

Notes left in the church and addressed to God directly or through one of the icons reveal both the sincerity and the confidence of the people. Most people do not ask for much, and they readily express their confidence that God will listen and understand. Notes left in the past at the feet of the Black Christ of Esquipulas contained the following requests:

Jesus, the man I'm living with is no good. He doesn't love my child. Help me to find a man that will love me and my child and if not me, at least my child.

Father in heaven, they just took my son to jail. Help him to be released soon. Let the guards and other prisoners have compassion for him.

Jesus, make my supervisor at work be more understanding and help me to get the next promotion which I really need to keep my kids in a Catholic school.

Please bring this neat guy I chased away back into my life. Why do I have to be so quick-tempered and foul-mouthed?

A year ago I was desperate because of the bad effects caused by the medicines I was taking. Crying and mortified I came to you for help. You, my suffering Black Christ, understood me. You did not leave me alone and brought about a miracle in me. I will never stop thanking you. Please never leave me alone.

Jesus, help the officials understand that I am entitled to Medicare and Medicaid. They try to trick me and I cannot defend myself. I don't even understand what they are saying. Please help them understand. You have helped me before. Please do not leave me alone now for I am old and all alone except for you.

I arrived here a year ago with nothing. I still have hardly anything. I know I deserve nothing because I have sinned so much, but I know you love me and will help me. Don't let me lose hope. Help me not to give up.

The people of San Fernando may not have learned about God from theology or even basic catechesis, but they do know God personally. The intensity of their bodily presence leaves no doubt that they are in deep, mystical union with God. They may be the mystics of the streets or of the public housing units and the courtrooms or the jails. They may be unknown or ignored by the world, but they do know they are loved by God. Their messages left in the church say, "This is my Father's and Mother's home. Here I know beyond all doubt that I truly belong. They listen to me with care and concern, they understand me and do not condemn me, they correct me but do not destroy me, they forgive me, they heal me and give me strength, they love me as I am. What more can I ask?"

Their simple petitions from the heart are profound and moving revelations of the nature of the God who is alive and present in San Fernando. God is the understanding and loving parent who is anxious to listen to the cries of the children who—although they get themselves into trouble—love God and cry out for guidance and protection. For a people accustomed to being ignored by officials and authority, the silent listening of God is powerful and life-giving. With no fear of ridicule or judgment, they demonstrate their unquestioning confidence that God will listen with concern and tenderness. The silent, listening presence of God allows people to be themselves, to clarify their thoughts, to console their sorrows, to think of new ideas, to gain strength in the face of tiredness and countless frustrations. This is their source of strength, courage, and life.

The Voice of Supplication

The cathedral is often filled with people seeking help. Their water or electricity is going to be turned off; they are about to be evicted because they cannot pay the rent; they do not have diapers, milk, or formula for their children; they have to travel to get to a job or back home, and they cannot afford the repairs for their car; they do not have money for their medicine, glasses, or false teeth; they are undocumented and have nowhere to go; they are hungry and want just a bit to eat. Or they have been robbed through dirty but legal deals like balloon loans or uncompleted repairs on a home that leave it worse than before. They are often the victims of legal robbery by people

who take advantage of the defenseless, especially undocumented immigrants and the poor, by promising them "papers" or other services that they need. They cry to heaven for justice, for they know that God alone cares.

That they come begging for help is already a loud, prophetic cry for God's kingdom of justice to come into existence. Most of these supplicants are eager for honest work to support themselves and their families. Often their children go to school without breakfast, and the entire family survives on a minimum of food. Some petitioners may stand by the cathedral doors looking for a hand-out. While others complain that this "looks bad," a Christic presence is visible in their broken bodies and disfigured faces. Their prophetic voices and their very presence denounce the injustices of our society and reveal aspects of our way of life that we would rather not recognize or admit. They remind us that as good as our society might be, much remains to be done to eliminate poverty and misery. As long as there are people who have to beg for their daily bread, the kingdom of God is not fully present.

FIESTA OF PRAISE

While the people of San Fernando express and exhibit their pains quite openly, they also sing out their joy which transcends all suffering. Such music is an essential component of San Fernando's life. Traditional music puts parishioners in continuity with their ancestors and allows them to participate in a very personal way in the communion of the saints. The words are the essence of their collective faith, and the rhythms provide a sort of life-giving continuum. Both words and rhythms come from the past and hold the present to the future.

San Fernando has several excellent yet very diverse choirs. What they all have in common is that the music is sung with deep conviction and expresses—regardless of the language or rhythm—the contagious joy of the people. At San Fernando, traditional music encompasses Native American chants and drum, the Latin High Mass, European classical composers such as Mozart and Handel, mariachi, and Spanish colonial hymns. To this are added popular Mexican-American songs and new songs composed by parishioners, including a number of litanies that help us reflect upon our own lives. At times, different forms of music are combined to form a distinctive San Fernando tradition. The Spanish colonial *"Entren Santos Peregrinos"* has been converted to mariachi music and given a rock-like tempo. Western cowboy music has been combined with Mexican *corridos* to create a new, distinctly Tejano music in praise of God. Members have also composed new litanies, such as those of Joseph and Mary the Migrants. These litanies help worshipers reflect upon their own lives through what Jesus, Joseph, and Mary endured in their earthly existence.

The music performed by San Fernando's choirs praises God with deep conviction. Whether in Latin, Christian rock, or mariachi, the songs express several pervasive themes. Many hymns, known by heart and learned from the ancestors, connect the people of today with the past and assure the continuity of life. For several generations, the opening hymn of the Sunday High Mass has been *"Tu Reinarás"* (You Will Reign). This popular traditional song reveals the very soul and sustaining spirit of the Hispanic people.

> Christ will reign and finally we will have peace and abundance.
> His cross will be our flag and his love our only law.
> He will always reign because our nation belongs to Mary.

By recognizing the true king and ruler, the one freely and joyfully acclaimed, San Fernando confesses its true and ultimate identity. By allowing Christ and Mary to reign in bodies, hearts, and souls, worshipers become aware that, regardless of what anyone says about them, they are truly God's people, a royal people, a chosen people—and thus inferior to no one.

A new song that quickly captured the hearts of the people is *"Pescador"* (Fisher of People). This life-giving song affirms and assures us that each person is called by name, in a very tender and personal way, to follow Jesus on the way of discipleship.

> You have come not searching intelligent and rich ones,
> You only want for me to follow you.
> You have looked into my eyes,
> Smiling, you have called my name.
> I have left my boat on the sand,
> With you I will seek another sea.

> You need my hands,
> May my weariness give rest to others,
> May my love continue loving.

Together, these two songs illuminate the roots of the basic character and personality of the people of San Fernando; Jesus reigns, calls them by name, and invites them to follow him so as to love as he has loved—without limit or barrier.

Another theme expressed in San Fernando's music is praise for Mary. Each day at San Fernando usually begins by singing *"Buenos Dias Paloma Blanca"* (Good Morning, My White Dove). Traditionally, Latinos wake people up with song to brighten the day. There seems no more beautiful way to begin the day (and worship) than by greeting Mary, the common mother who is the very source and sustenance of life, the beloved "dove" who is invoked in the popular prayer of the people that she might "illuminate the Holy Spirit." Indeed, it is the sense of the faithful that even the Holy Spirit needs help.

One new song to Mary adopted by San Fernando is *"Santa María del Camino"* (Holy Mary of the Way). In the words of this song of courage, Mary is not just a pacifier, but one who helps to animate the struggles for justice and a new humanity. Mary gives strength and courage. As she illuminates the Holy Spirit, she also illuminates people's imaginations to dream dreams others have not dared to pursue.

> Even though some will tell you nothing can change,
> Struggle for a new world, and others will follow you.
> Come walk with us, Mary, come walk with us.

Each day or major celebration ends by saying "goodbye" to our mother, our queen in the words of *"Adios Reina del Cielo"* and *"Adios O Virgen de Guadalupe."* In Spanish, it is very common to call beloved women *mi reina* (my queen). This expression is used for daughters, mothers, wives, and lovers. *Mi reina* is not the queen who rules with power but the queen who has captured hearts with her love, tenderness, and compassion. The relationship of the parishioners with Mary is a very personal and personalizing one that is continually reinforced and deepened by words (*mi reina* and *mi mamacita*) and music. Mary dispels loneliness and fear because she is always present for the people, and the image of Mary as the common mother of all connects people with one another. Abstract titles for Mary have little import at San Fernando, for the people know her personally as the true mother in the flesh.

A third theme of hymns at San Fernando and in other Mexican communities is a very realistic sense of human sinfulness, not because people are bad, but because they are human. Sinfulness is part of the human condition. During confession, people often use the phrase, "*Pues, Padre, es la naturaleza*" (Well, Father, it is nature). This is not a matter of ignoring sin, or of excusing it lightly, or of glorifying it, but of admitting it before God and one another.

Acknowledgments of both personal and collective sin are prominent, particularly during the Lenten season and especially during the Good Friday processions, when parishioners sing "*Perdona Tu Pueblo, Señor*" and "*Perdón, O Dios Mio*" with one voice from the depths of their being. The first hymn is an ancient Lenten song that is a collective request for forgiveness as a people. It acknowledges that sinfulness lies at the very roots of our historical and cultural existence. We are not perfect or without fault. We do things we do not want to do. We do not brag about this, but neither do we deny it. The second hymn, "*Perdón, O Dios Mio*," is a deep and anguished request for personal forgiveness. Not only am I part of a sinful people, but I personally have sinned and need God's forgiveness.

Throughout the year San Fernando celebrates the triumph of the cross, the triumph of enduring love over the violence of human beings and humanity itself. Hymns such as "*Victoria, Tu Reinarás, O Cruz, Tu Nos Salvarás*" (The Victory of the Cross That Will Save Us) and "*Venid O Cristianos la Cruz Adoremos, la Cruz Ensalcemos Que al Mundo Salvó*" (Come, Christians, Let Us Adore the Cross Through Which the World Was Saved) are sung beautifully and passionately by the people of San Fernando. In the suffering of today and of past generations, it is the suffering Savior who accompanies us on our multiple journeys and struggles for survival and life. He is with us when we cross the border, risking the abuse of Mexican gangs or U.S. border patrols. He is present in the daily way of the cross at work, at school, or even at home. It is the suffering Savior who enables us to withstand insults and injuries and to continue forward with the full dignity and unquestioned confidence of the children of God. Thus, we rise above any type of disaster or suffering and sing out with the greatest confidence and joy about the triumph of the cross, the triumph of accompaniment, the triumph of endurance.

This deep sense of Christ's abiding presence, especially in the Eucharist, is another popular theme of hymns. Two songs that emphasize this theme and are popular all year, but especially on Holy Thursday, are *"Cantemos al Amor de los Amores"* (Let Us Sing to the Love of All Loves) and *"Alabado Sea el Santísimo"* (Praise Be the Most Holy Sacrament). Through the Blessed Sacrament Jesus is present for each individual personally and for all of us collectively.

A song whose words are at the origins of Christianity itself but whose melody is quite new is *"Padre Nuestro."* It was written by one of our local San Antonio composers, Carlos Rosas. The melody captures the deep collective soul of the people, and its rhythm celebrates a sense of extended family and peoplehood. As people join hands and sing this song, a mystical unity is experienced by everyone present, including even viewers of San Fernando's international telecasts. Catholics of all ethnic backgrounds, Protestants of many denominations, people of other religions, and even atheists have experienced this unity, the incredible feeling that millions of people at one moment in time are holding on to each other, accompanying and supporting one another, as they sing of the common loving parenthood of God for the entire human race.

One of the most popular songs at San Fernando, *"De Colores,"* which became well known through the Cursillo movement, celebrates life and is appropriate for all festive occasions. The words describe the flowers of various colors, the songs of the birds, the crow of the cocks, the *qui-qui-ri-ki-ki* of the chickens, the colors of the rainbow, and so on. In its simple but poetic way, it proclaims the joy and illumination of conversion, the ability to see and experience everything and everyone in a radically new and exciting way. This, indeed, is what the people of San Fernando experience through praising God with music. Music allows one to see, understand, and appreciate all creation—every person and each situation—in a new way, in God's way. Even if the world has not actually changed or the people in the next pew or living next door have not changed, the faithful can see them anew, and this is why they rejoice.

6

THE GOSPEL UNVEILED
AND PROCLAIMED

Virgilio P. Elizondo

The sermon pulls all the voices of the people together and reinterprets them through the light of the gospel readings of the day. From our present situation, we turn to the gospel for clarification, meaning, motivation, and sustenance. As our own stories take on new significance and direction, we also rediscover aspects of the Word of God. This exciting mutuality of interpretation between our human situation and the gospel becomes actualized each day through the sermon.

In the cathedral, the proclamation of the Word of God does not begin when the preacher mounts the lectern to preach. Instead, it begins with the very first word of welcome one hears on arriving at the cathedral, and it continues through the entire liturgical celebration. The formal "homily" makes explicit and brings together what the people have already been experiencing. From the actual moment of entering the cathedral, the ushers make everyone feel at home. "We are so glad you are here. You honor us with your presence." The ushers are neither intimidated by the famous and powerful who enter nor are they scandalized by the poor and neglected. At San Fernando everyone is important and precious.

It is not just the ushers who put worshipers at ease. The regular parishioners have a style of presence that immediately makes others feel comfortable and welcome. Before our televised Mass, we remind our parishioners that all of us together are the message we are about to transmit. No one is less important than the presider or the choir, even if the presider is the bishop or the pope. We ask people to introduce themselves to each other before the Mass, and we remind them that it is not a sin to enjoy our religious celebration. I often wonder where Christians got the idea that church and worship should not be enjoyed, when the greatest characteristic of the first Christians was their spontaneous and very visible joy.

The first parts of worship lead to one of the principal moments of our celebrations and parish life—the sermon. Without the living word that invites, helps, and challenges people to growth in faith, everything else could quickly degenerate into mere folklore or correct but empty ritual. Without meaningful and inspiring sermons, San Fernando could become a kind of living museum of ancient rituals. The sermon proclaims God's clarifying, piercing, recreating, and life-giving Word.

San Fernando sermons try to make explicit and clarify what all of us attempt to live out in our daily contacts with others. We believe that the word of God is not just a word about the past, but the all-important word for today. We begin where Jesus started, with the actual struggles, questions, and unsuspected "idols" of the people around him. The crowds that gathered around him questioned him constantly about their religion, their society, their faith. In our contemporary situation, we try to clarify, purify, deepen, and amplify the meaning and challenge of God's word in today's world.

The key themes of preaching at San Fernando draw on the humanity of Jesus. It is this humanity that reveals to us both the true nature of God's divinity and the true meaning of human life, so that our humanity takes on new purpose and meaning. We make a clear option for a Christianity that emerges from the full meaning of the Incarnation. As recent popes and the new *Catechism of the Catholic Church* have stated, every aspect of Jesus' life and message is crucial and basic to our preaching and pastoral life. Through the telling of the earthly identity, life, and mission of this man from Galilee, we hope the people will come to know and love in an ever deeper way the character and personality of God, the God who takes on our flesh and skin, our voice and language, our social and religious status, our *mestizaje* and marginalization. We talk often of Jesus, who, like us, was of a mixed, impure race—"the stone rejected by the builders"—but who was also the chosen foundation stone for the new creation. The new creation triumphs over human divisiveness to form a new

and all-inclusive human family. We understand that although salvation is for all eternity, it begins nevertheless in the here and now.

Our sermons emphasize themes of particular importance, not only to our congregation, but to all humanity.

The Basic Dignity and Infinite Worth of the Human Being

For God so loved the world that he gave his only Son, so that everyone who believes in him might not perish but might have eternal life. (John 3:16)

The very core of Christianity is that we are treasured, even in our sinfulness, that God loves us so much that he sent his son to give his life for us. Despite our sinfulness, the divine in us has not been lost, even if it seems hidden at times. From the instant of our conception, each one of us is so precious and so important that we are worth dying for. If each of us is that important and valuable to God, we must be equally valuable to our own selves and to others; similarly, others must be equally valuable to us.

The story of the Samaritan woman at the well is a powerful illustration of this theme. Ostracized by others, she was befriended by Jesus, because despite everything she had done, she was a human being, a beloved creature of God. Because Jesus befriended her, she became one of the very first witnesses of the new life offered by Jesus. Jesus didn't ask her to convert, he simply engaged her in a very personal and friendly conversation.

This message of human dignity and worth is one that people need to hear, especially people who struggle with demeaning situations. One woman wrote, "I used to be a prostitute because I thought I was worthless and that no one liked me. Selling myself made me feel desired. Ever since I started coming to San Fernando, I experienced such love, even though the people knew what my profession had been, that now I am happily working at something else."

Children are welcomed and regarded as having the same worth and dignity as adults. Because we have no separate classrooms, our catechism classes have to take place in the sanctuary. Each Saturday morning, the church is packed with children studying about Jesus.

They sing, pray, talk, and play. Yes, at times they are loud, but they do find great joy in the house of the Lord.

Each Person Is Someone Special, Basically Good, and Loved by God

Look at the birds in the sky; they do not sow or reap, they gather noth-ing into barns, yet your heavenly Father feeds them. Are not you more important than they? (Matthew 6:26)

A second theme focuses on the need to give people a new appreci-ation of themselves, each other, their families, the stranger and for-eigner, the immigrants, our city, society, and God. In spite of our sin-fulness, in spite of our attempts to destroy ourselves, in spite of what others say about us, we are good. Sin blinds us from seeing the good, and sin makes the evil attractive and appealing. Freedom from sin allows us to see and appreciate the good—in ourselves and in oth-ers—that has been hidden from us.

One of the most devastating sins can be the failure to recognize our talents, our potential, and the goodness that is within each one of us, even the worst sinner. An underestimation of self, the conviction that "we are not as good," can be the greatest sin of poor people and oppressed minorities and can lead to paralyzing feelings of inferiority. Discovering the good, the true, and the beautiful within us, which we have not suspected and which society has denied or ignored, is one of the greatest life-giving experiences. This is a call to conversion. In the words of one man, "I like to come to San Fernando because the ser-mons put you in contact with those good aspects of yourself that you had not suspected. You feel so good about yourself that you can't wait to get out there and live out these good aspects that are so beautiful."

God Needs Each of Us

[Jesus] said to them, "There is no need for them to go away; give them some food yourselves." (Matthew 14:16)

Another sin is that poor and oppressed minorities have been told so often and in so many ways that they are inferior and have nothing to offer society except cheap labor, that they have begun to believe this. Over time, they become convinced of it. They often underestimate their potential, feel inferior in the presence of people from the dominant culture, and are convinced that others must teach them and correct them. When people are released from this form of bondage and begin to appreciate and enjoy their talents and abilities, liberation and life begin.

The church has impoverished itself immensely because it has not invited people as they are into the active and creative ministry of the church. Often, an emphasis on orthodoxy and ordained ministry has prevented the faithful from appreciating and developing the God-given talents that they can contribute to the life of the church and society.

Break Barriers of Separation

Jesus stretched out his arm, touched him [the leper] and said: "I do will it, be made clean." (Matthew 8:3)

The lepers were legally unclean people at the time of Jesus. They were kept apart from the community, and anyone who touched them incurred uncleanness and would likewise be separated from the community. Leprosy was one of those absolute barriers that kept some people totally separated from the others. Jesus could have healed at a distance, as he did on other occasions, but instead he chose to break social and religious barriers and physically touch the untouchable to make him clean. That barriers should not exist between people is an important message that is often heard in the pulpit of San Fernando.

The Importance of Peacemaking and Discipleship

Blessed are the peacemakers for they shall be called children of God. (Matthew 5:9)

Sermons encourage people to take an active part in neighborhood organizations, school boards, political elections, and other projects that will improve the quality of life for everyone. We encourage people to take active stands on controversial issues, such as immigration

issues and the status and treatment of the undocumented, meals for school children, and workers' benefits. Unfortunately, active peace-making often involves painful confrontations, like those Jesus had with the authorities of his day. We tell the people, though, that when such confrontations are necessary, they should not be avoided.

The gospel makes us free so we can work for peace through seeking justice and showing compassion. We are called to unmask and confront the injustice of our society. Working in the world to bring about new structures of justice, dignity, and equality is the privileged ministry of the Christian laity. This is not an easy or popular task, but one that needs to be sustained and nourished with the spirituality of discipleship.

One of the greatest challenges to peacemaking is domestic violence in the home. The first school for learning loving relationships should be the home. This is where one should learn to tolerate difference, to get along with each other, to forgive, to share, to work together. Children should be loved and sacrificed for, as Christ did for us. But building a domestic community of love and compassion does not happen automatically; in today's world it has to be worked at to be achieved.

Power of Prayer

"Lord, teach us to pray. . . . " (Luke 11:1)

The style of prayer is quite secondary. The important thing is to realize our absolute dependence upon prayer, whether personal or communal, whether spontaneous or rote, whether form-prayer or simple conversation or even the prayer of silence. Whatever the style, we must develop an attitude of prayer so that we allow and welcome God into all the affairs of our lives.

When preaching on the Lord's Prayer, we also emphasize the values of family life that are so needed today. Due to pressures from popular culture and society, family life is constantly threatened with decay and dissolution. Both fatherhood and motherhood need to be promoted in their fullness, including the spiritual role to be played by the father in the family.

Radical and Unconditional Forgiveness

"Father, forgive them, they know not what they do." (Luke 23:34)

"If your brother sins, rebuke him; and if he repents, forgive him. And if he wrongs you seven times in one day and returns to you seven times saying, 'I am sorry,' you should forgive him." (Luke 17:3-4)

Only by forgiving can we become free. Resentment is enslavement, and forgiveness is freedom. We should never forget that the church is the fellowship of acknowledged sinners who recognize and rejoice in the confident assurance that we have been cleansed, saved, and healed by God's grace and not by any merit of ours. This grace becomes visible through our joyous forgiveness and acceptance of one another. It is precisely through our human weakness that God's power and glory is made manifest.

Presence of a Loving Mother

"Then he said to the disciple, 'Behold, your mother.'" (John 19:27)

"You have nothing to fear, am I not here, your merciful and loving mother?" (From the narrative of Our Lady of Guadalupe to Juan Diego)

Mary, the mother of suffering humanity, has a very special role in the life and preaching of San Fernando. Under the titles of *Nuestra Señora de la Candelaria* and Our Lady of Guadalupe, she is the patroness of the parish. We are never ashamed or apologetic about our love of Mary. Our devotion includes her historical role as Our Lady of Guadalupe, a significant image for the many *mestizo* people at San Fernando, and also her biblical role as Mary of Nazareth, the accompanying and life-giving Galilean mother of Jesus who, at the cross, became the mother of all disciples. Like a great jewel, she does not appear too often in the gospels, but when she appears it is always at core moments in the life of Jesus. It almost seems as if the gospels are trying to tell us that Jesus could not have accomplished his work without his mother.

The Joy of Fellowship

"They ate their meals with exultation and sincerity of heart, praising God and enjoying favor with all the people. And every day the Lord added to the number of those who were being saved." (Acts 2:46-47)

The joyfulness and sincerity of San Fernando's Sunday and festive celebrations attract people from all walks of life and from various religions. We constantly remind our parishioners that church is to be enjoyed, that enjoying worship is not sinful. We should be like children in our parents' home, with a joyfulness that irrupts from the depths of the family's love and concern for one another and the pleasure of being together. Our joy and happiness should attract others to enter and experience it as well.

The worship language of San Fernando, like any living language, has been shaped and conditioned by memories, tradition, the contemporary situation, and especially by the Word of God. The language of the people of San Fernando is characterized by their honesty, simplicity, spontaneity, joy, and unquestioned confidence in the God who listens, cares, and comes to our rescue. It is the language of people who have been stepped on, but never crushed; humiliated, but not humbled; deprived and robbed of many things and opportunities, but not of life itself; ignored, but not silenced. Although they have been kept out of many places, God has not been kept out of them. It is the language of God's children who, with a great sense of gratitude, pride, and self-confidence, speak and sing the praises of the God who is glorified in all of us.

7

THE SACRED IN THE CITY

Virgilio P. Elizondo

"San Fernando keeps alive the memories of our childhood, of our ancestors. It keeps our Mexican soul alive and lets us feel at home. People come here because here they can be who they are."

The soul is the life of a person, of a movement, a city, a nation, a people. It is the mysterious but very real life-source that makes the difference between life and death and that defines the individuality and quality of a particular life. The collective rituals of San Fernando—with their traditional songs, gestures, statues, and decorations—are the very soul of San Fernando, the representation of the inner life and ultimate identity of its people. People participate in these rituals not just from religious obligation but because they want to in the innermost fiber of their being.

Public rituals are a collective way of experiencing God in which all the people act and appear as one body, the body of Christ. This is a gathering of *un pueblo*, a people of one mind and heart, intimately interconnected through the ritual itself. Each individual is an integral part of the ritual, yet the full ritual is beyond and outside of any person. As a visiting theologian observed, "This experience affirms and enlarges the identity of the person, allowing each one to find a greater sense of self."

The ritual might be processing with palms, walking up with others to receive ashes, heartfelt singing of the *mañanitas* to Our Lady of Guadalupe, or following Jesus along the way of the cross. The act of walking together with a collective focus on the object of the ritual brings everyone to a particular location at a specific moment in time. As each person participates in the ritual, he or she is carried by the very movement of the ritual, all walking, singing, praying, reflecting, responding as one person.

This is not the unity of a military unit or even the unity of a monastic group praying in perfect uniformity of purpose, dress, gesture, and song where the individual is totally subsumed by the group. Instead, the public faith rituals of San Fernando bring together an incredible diversity of people—the faithful of all ages and backgrounds, tourists, passers-by, the curious. All barriers of exclusion dissolve into a profound communion that is experienced by everyone who participates. When public rituals take place in the Market Square at the heart of San Antonio, whoever is present for whatever reason is invited into the group without any feeling of being coerced or forced to conform. Visitors seem to have a deep sense of belonging and often forget they are visitors or foreigners because they feel themselves part of the family. One time even a crimson-robed cardinal from the Vatican simply blended into the crowd. Everyone who approaches and joins in experiences the deep bond of belonging. The very magnetic force of the ritual seems to pull people in.

Through these religious rituals, each person experiences the truth of the past here and now in a very active way by actually reliving the events that have given life to all of us. In the common experience we all see, hear, feel, and relive our collective birth and development as a people. It is in these moments that our deepest cultural identity is affirmed. We are reborn through Jesus of Nazareth and recreated into a particular people of God, a *mestizo* people with deep roots but without borders, with great memories but without resentment, with many hurts but great love. A visiting liturgist described this as "an affectionate experience of God that totally consumes me. Among all the noise and distractions of the downtown traffic, there is a deep quietness that drowns out the noises. All the defenses are gone, and we all experience God."

RITUAL AND *MESTIZO* CHRISTIANITY

The faith of Mexican Americans today results from the gradual synthesis of the Catholic religion of the Spanish colonizers and the spiritual practices of the Indians, who were already deeply religious peoples. Our basic identity continues to be a great synthesis—*mestizaje*—that started in 1519 with the initial military and spiritual conquest of Mexico and the anthropological birth of *mestizo* America. A second synthesis occurred when Catholic Mexicans encountered the Protestant Anglo-Saxons from the United States and the European Catholics who settled in Texas. The third *mestizaje* is taking place today in the encounter with modernity and fundamentalism. Yet, throughout all these *mestizajes*, our original Indian roots continue to inform and influence our identity and core values.

To understand and appreciate our *mestizo* Christian celebrations, it is important to note that everything—including all people and all events—is deeply interconnected. The full meaning of our religious rituals lies in the profound belief in the triumph of life over death, both throughout our lives and after our deaths. In that sense, all our important celebrations are paschal, because they are part of the continuum of the great Passover of Jesus.

LA PASCUA GUADALUPANA (THE FEAST OF OUR LADY OF GUADALUPE)

It is difficult for those who do not have Mexican roots to fully appreciate or understand the deep personal meaning and power of this feast. We Mexican Americans are partly to blame for this. Because it is such a foundational feast for us and because we have never needed any explanation for it to be meaningful, we have neither explored its fascinating place in the history of salvation of the Americas nor sought to share it with others in a serious way. We have allowed it to remain as a "pious Mexican feast" rather than celebrating it for what it really is—the feast of the spiritual birth of the Americas.

The year 1521, when the humanities of the two halves of the planet finally met, marked the beginning of the collective crucifixion of the innocent victims of the Americas at the hands of the colonizers. It appeared that the gods of the indigenous peoples had deserted them, and they were alone with absolutely no one to understand them or protect them. However, only ten years later an event took place that was to change the course of history. Guadalupe, the brown-skinned woman who appeared to the peasant Juan Diego at

Tepeyac, the site of the ancient goddess Tonantzin, spoke to the defeated and humiliated Indians with tenderness and respect. She recognized their dignity and importance, and she asked them to be her partner in an important enterprise of God. Speaking in the language of the defeated, with their poetry and imagery, she made it evident that it was God speaking through her.

In and through Guadalupe, God raised to life what the invading armies had killed, crushed, and humiliated. December 12, the day of the apparition of Our Lady of Guadalupe, is the most festive day of the year at San Fernando. For us, Guadalupe is like the risen Lord explaining the scriptures to the disciples on the way to Emmaus. Guadalupe opens a new way of understanding the full meaning of this life-giving event.

This day's celebrations are the oldest and most traditional of all the fiestas in and around San Fernando, and they are also the most colorful and the most lively. The festival is a twenty-four-hour celebration that begins the evening of December 11 when the best-known singers of the community gather together to sing their tribute to Guadalupe, our mother and the source of our being. Singing and dancing mark this celebration of our origins and our resurrection. At midnight, all gather together to sing the first *mañanitas* (birthday greetings). The *mañanitas* are sung again a little later, just before the break of day. This sunrise service symbolizes the beginning of the new day of the Americas, when a new light breaks forth.

Throughout the entire day, families and individuals visit our image of Guadalupe, *La Morenita del Tepeyac*. Some bring flowers, others sing to her, and still others simply pay their respects. The long celebration ends that evening with a communal service like a living rosary. In between the mysteries, each person in the church has the opportunity to deposit a flower at Our Lady's feet. At this moment they touch her, and they are touched by her. Their eyes and their entire facial expressions leave no doubt at all that they are in personal contact with the divine and that very intimate communication takes place between the maternal divine and her human children. It is fascinating to note that a great number of men of all ages and appearances participate with profound devotion and conviction, a public display of faith rarely visible in seminaries or religious houses.

LA PASCUA NAVIDEÑA (THE BIRTH OF OUR LORD)

As Guadalupe marks the beginning of *mestizo* Christianity, so the birth of the Messiah marks the beginning of the divine-human *mestizaje*. It is the entry of God into the flesh of human history and into our own particular historical journey. Mexican-American Christians are fascinated with the *niño Dios* (child God) and all the historical events surrounding the Christmas story, from the annunciation to the arrival of the three kings.

One of the favorite celebrations of the people also comes yearly at Christmas time. *Las posadas* recreate on nine evenings the journey of Joseph and Mary to Bethlehem. In this simple neighborhood ritual, families gather together and parade from house to house carrying *El Misterio,* statues of Joseph and Mary riding on the donkey. At each house they ask for shelter and are turned away. Finally, they are welcomed and a small fiesta takes place. Sometimes participants in the *posada* pray the rosary or read from scripture. Their procession through the neighborhood is accompanied by traditional singing and the repetition of the Litany of Migrants. The litany, composed by the people, recalls the many insults and abuses migrants have to face each day. The response to the litany is, "With Joseph and Mary, pilgrims keep on walking."

On one of these nine nights, a *gran posada* begins in Market Square in the middle of San Antonio and makes its way through the historic section, visiting various merchants, the old Governor's Palace, City Hall, the County Court House. Refused entry at each place, the *posada* finally arrives at the cathedral where the large crowd is welcomed with festive singing and a party with gifts for all present.

The *posadas* climax on the night of December 24 when the procession arrives at the crib to enthrone the child Jesus. This *acostada del niño* and the adoration of the Christ Child at the end of Mass are the highlights of the night. Everyone in the congregation is given an opportunity to go forward to kiss the baby Jesus. Of course, everyone knows this is only a statue, but for them—for us—what we are really kissing is the real Christ Child mystically present in the plastic one. The sanctuary has been converted into a life-size Bethlehem scene, and traditional Spanish Christmas music enhances a festive, emotional, and glorious Mass.

Another significant moment of Christmas is when the three kings arrive to distribute gifts for all the children in honor of the Christ Child. Finally, the feasts surrounding *la pascua navideña* end with the presentation of the Christ Child in the temple. All parents with children under one year are asked to bring their babies to church so that they, like the child Jesus, might be offered to God. During the offertory all the parents gather around the altar and offer their children to God. They also recommit themselves to being loving and responsible parents of the children that God has entrusted to their care. After this ritual, a floral offering is made in honor of the babies that died during their first year of life, and then a second offering of flowers is given for the babies that were conceived but were not born.

MIERCOLES DE CENIZA (ASH WEDNESDAY)

Ash Wednesday is a phenomenal day in the mosaic of feasts at San Fernando. The full meaning of this day seems beyond comprehension, but its impact is undeniable. Throughout the day, people of all ages and backgrounds arrive to receive ashes. Families bring their infants in arms and their elderly in wheelchairs. Usually around twelve hundred people come through the cathedral each half hour. Even though confessions are heard throughout the day and communion is offered, it is the ashes that people seek. They leave within a few minutes of their arrival, proudly displaying the ashes on their foreheads. As people see them on the street, they rush to the church to get their ashes.

What is the attraction of the ashes? A sign of communion with the earth? A reminder of our mortality? A public confession that we are all sinners in need of repentance? An affirmation of our existence as human beings? It is all of these, but for the Christians of San Antonio, and Mexican Americans in particular, the deep signification of the ashes (dust to dust) can be found in a history of suffering, marginalization, and displacement at the hands of colonizers, power holders, land holders, and immigration patrols. Ash Wednesday is a painful recognition of history, a prophetic denunciation of the unjust structures that cause it, and a proud and determined proclamation that *mestizaje* people are here to stay. Bringing children to receive the ashes assures that this heritage will live on in generations to come.

Forced to live like the dust, without earth to hold it in place, we know that the earth is ours. In receiving ashes with respect, determination, and joy, we proclaim to ourselves and to others that *así es la vida* (such is life), that we will not give up or surrender, but we will continue to proclaim the joy of living with our songs, rituals, and festivals.

DOMINGO DE RAMOS (PALM SUNDAY)

The triumphant entry of Jesus into Jerusalem marks our very own triumphant entry into the structures of society. During the solemn blessing of the palms in the middle of Main Street, thousands of people gather together, waving palms and singing Hosannas, as the procession clearly affirms the legitimacy of our existence and our determination to enter into the social structures that condition and govern our lives.

The procession is religious but certainly not "churchy." Cars are passing by, tourists look on in curiosity or awe, people jump out of the bus to join the procession, vendors try to make a little money by selling the traditional *manzanilla* (chamomile tea) and woven palms. The crowd acts as one person as they truly walk with Jesus. This journey into the heart of San Antonio is a living experience of the entry into Jerusalem.

JUEVES SANTO (HOLY THURSDAY)

In our *mestizo* tradition, the rituals of Holy Week allow the present generation to see, smell, touch, hear, and taste the events that gave rise to the tradition. They are thus free to experience the guidance of the spirit in arriving at their own contemporary interpretations.

Holy Thursday begins with a procession to the cenacle, the room where Jesus and his disciples shared their last meal. On this evening, the sanctuary resembles a dining room with worshipers dressed as they think people dressed at the time of Jesus. When the gospel of the washing of the feet is read, the archbishop removes his vestments, puts a towel around his waist and proceeds to wash the feet of the men dressed as apostles. By this very gesture, he—and Jesus himself—is identifying with typical jobs held by Mexican Americans, jobs that society often considers degrading—dishwashing, shoe shining,

windshield washing on street corners—and showing the dignity that lies in the service of others.

After the Mass of the Last Supper, in which the bread is blessed for distribution to the people, the entire congregation leaves the church in a candlelight procession through Main Plaza. During this symbolic walk to the Garden of Gethsemane, worshipers sing a litany based on the humanity of Jesus with the response, "Let us walk with Jesus." The procession is solemn, yet very real as, without fail, there are always hecklers shouting insults, curious tourists, a prostitute waiting for customers, an occasional drunk who may be moved to tears, cars honking, astonished bystanders. Observers wonder what we are about, but the people in the procession have no doubts as they continue to sing, *"Caminemos con Jesús"* (Let us walk with Jesus).

When the procession returns to the cathedral, the sanctuary has been transformed into the Garden of Gethsemane. As the Blessed Sacrament is reposed, the people sing traditional songs handed down over generations, including *"Alabado sea el Santísimo, Sacramento del Altar."* After a few moments of silent adoration, people are invited to come during the night to spend some time in silent prayer with Jesus, just as he invited the disciples to keep him company. This is the night when each person can be alone with Jesus. The adoration continues until midnight, the traditional hour of Jesus' arrest, when the liturgy moves naturally into the beginning of Good Friday.

VIERNES SANTO (GOOD FRIDAY)

At midnight the men of the parish gather to build the *calvario*. Their deep spirituality, as they move statues, decorate, and clean up, makes these actions a vital part of the liturgy, rather than simply preparation or setting the stage. The experience of this entire liturgy, from building the *calvario* to burial, is a phenomenon that defies explanation. For those who experience it, it is a deeply human and sacred moment. Indeed, the entire twenty-four-hour liturgy is permeated by a mood of reflection and prayer.

The day begins around eight o'clock in the morning when the men and women of the parish gather to dress for the Passion proclamation. There are no professional actors, only ordinary believers who will live a part for the day. The simple costumes are made by the people themselves. In an atmosphere of excitement and deep reverence, the people gather together in prayer to remind the participants that their mission is to help everyone experience both the extent of human malice and the infinite dimensions of God's love through Jesus; we recall that we are not staging a drama, but leading people into a human experience of the sacred.

At the *Mercado,* the old Market Square of San Antonio, stages have been set up for Pilate and Herod and the crowd of thousands has assembled. At ten o'clock the trumpet sounds and a centurion announces that Pilate will hear the case against the so-called Jesus of Nazareth. From this point, the words and movements follow the gospel accounts of the Passion. Pilate presents Jesus to the people, hoping that the crowd will take pity, but the crowd demands the cross.

Wearing a crown of thorns and accompanied by a traditional song, *"Perdona Tu Pueblo, Señor,"* Jesus begins to carry his cross through the streets of San Antonio. As the crowd follows the Galilean, the Mercado area, usually full of tourists and music, is completely transformed. This is not a church service or a parade or a political demonstration or an orderly procession of clergy, religious, and pious folks. There are no casual observers because even the reporters become participants in the living drama.

Then, in front of La Margarita, one of San Antonio's favorite restaurants, Jesus falls for the first time. The crowd stops, the singing stops. There is a profound silence. A woman in the balcony sings the famous song, "I Don't Know How to Love Him," from *Jesus Christ Superstar.* No explanation is needed, for through her song to the fallen and bloody Jesus we all confess our deepest feelings.

The march continues. Slowly Jesus stands up and moves forward with the cross. The shouts and insults of the soldiers are so real that they have even drawn blows and insults for their cruelty from onlookers. As Roman soldiers in their shining red capes and armor lead the group onto Dolorosa Street (the actual Via Dolorosa of San Antonio), Jesus falls a second time. One year a young boy broke away from his mother and ran to wipe the face of Jesus with his handkerchief tenderly and to kiss him. Another small child called out to his mother, "Mommy, call the police, that's wrong! They can't just hit him like that!"

The archbishop of San Antonio takes on the role of Simon of

Cyrene. With great simplicity, he carries the cross, and his face communicates more than any sermon. He is burdened not by the physical weight of the cross, but the weight of the suffering of the world, the church, the people. As he walks slowly, bent over under the weight of the cross, he seems to say, "This is truly what being a follower of Jesus is all about; this is truly the authentic identity and mission of a bishop."

The media become part of the re-enactment. During the walk, reporters and cameramen become more intense. Each one wants to get closer, get a better shot, a more piercing sound, an emotional sound-bite. Although they cover the event every year, it is as if they had never been there before. Although it happened almost two thousand years ago, thousands of miles away, it is reported as if it happened for the very first time right in our own city. One television reporter said, "Today I committed the great sin of any reporter. I became so personally involved in what was taking place that I lost some of my best shots. But I recorded them in my heart and they will probably be the best shots I have ever taken!"

At midday the crowd passes through the Justice Center and arrives at the Main Plaza where the crucifixion will take place. Thousands of people are gathered, waiting in breathless silence with their eyes fixed in one direction. Then, as Jesus is stripped and placed on the cross, the sound of the hammer driving in the nails sends chills through everyone. Because the nails appear to be real and the shouts of Jesus are so agonizing, some people believe that this man is really being nailed to the cross.

As the cross is lifted at high noon with Jesus nailed to it, no one moves or even seems to blink. As Mary and the other women approach the cross, their cries of anguish and pain pierce each heart in the crowd, and men and women sob openly with them. The crowd has been transformed by the pain and agony of unjust cruelty. People know the helplessness of absolute powerlessness and utter a wordless protest while crying openly.

The insulting soldiers are now quiet, and suddenly, as if from the sky itself, the powerful voice of Jesus is heard, "Father, forgive them, for they know not what they do." When the final word is uttered, "Father, into your hands I commend my spirit," the only sound heard is the bell tolling the death of a fellow human being. It has ended.

The silent crowd waits. Then, one of the Roman soldiers proclaims the first confession of faith: "Truly, this was the Son of God." Then—as on the first Good Friday—the crowd slowly walks away.

In the sanctuary of the church the re-enactment becomes liturgical and ritual. As the choir in the church sings *"Tan solo que solo vas,"* the clergy, vested in crimson red, file slowly down the middle aisle. The people kneel. Each priest prostrates himself at the foot of the cross in a moment of profound, humble prayer. The solemn service begins with the crucified Jesus presiding. The clergy, including the archbishop, sit on a simple bench. Each scripture reading is followed by a brief sermon, a collective prayer, and a song. The church, the plaza, and its surroundings are crowded with people, but no one moves. All eyes and ears are fixed on the crucified. Throughout the afternoon, people keep coming to be with the crucified one who gave his life for all.

As the sun begins to set, gypsies, dressed in the black of mourning and wearing penitential hoods, arrive to take Jesus down from the cross. They sing lamentation songs while they slowly climb ladders and carefully remove the nails so that his arms collapse. Finally, the body is gently taken down and placed in the funeral litter. The singing continues as women dressed in black, and covered with traditional *mantillas,* anoint the body. The congregation spontaneously joins the lead singer in an unrehearsed lamentation of, *"Ay, ay, ay, ay, ay."* The burial procession moves down the middle aisle and out into the Main Plaza. With candles and torches, the congregation accompanies *La Soledad,* the solitary mother of Jesus, and the litter carrying his body through Soledad Street and Dolorosa Street, the two main streets around the cathedral that were named for the Good Friday procession. Eventually, the procession returns to the church, which for the night becomes the holy sepulcher.

The body is laid carefully in the center of the sanctuary. Now people begin to file by to pay their personal respects. Many bring simple flowers from their homes to put on the body of Jesus. They come, young and old, rich and poor, white, brown, and black, men with babies, people in wheelchairs, they just keep on coming and coming and coming. In the end, the body of Jesus is covered with a mountain of flowers. They kiss his feet, touch his face, feel his hands. The people's faces seem to ask, "Why? Did we have a part in this? Did we realize what we were doing? Was this killing necessary?"

It continues as people come to comfort *La Soledad*. Mary is no longer alone in her moment of sorrow. People who have suffered a particular crisis during the year come to share their pain with her: parents whose son committed suicide, a mother whose famous son has given grave public scandal, an archbishop who shares the pain of his sinful church. They speak for all of us, and we walk together in our sorrow, giving strength to one another. It is the very sharing of sorrows that gives us collective insight into the meaning of the crucifixion and its life-giving power. In the presence of the body, the mountain of flowers, and *La Soledad*, an inner peace begins to emerge within us. No more words are said, but everyone begins to leave slowly, knowing that a new life has indeed begun within us.

SABADO DE GLORIA (THE EASTER VIGIL)

Saturday is a day of silence filled with the tranquillity of nothingness. Then, at night, the commemoration of the unsuspected begins with a blaze of light. The fire is blessed, and the candle is lit to the singing of *"La luz de Jesús ha venido al mundo."* The readings call to mind the great interventions of God in history from the time of creation. Then when the resurrection of the crucified is proclaimed, the dark curtain that covers the entire sanctuary is opened, the lights go on, the trumpets sound, the organ plays, and children sing *"Ha resucitado"* (He is risen), as they throw flowers to the people. Following the announcement of the resurrection, the service celebrates the greatest intervention of God in history—the rebirth of sinners through baptism.

Then, the final liturgy, that of Easter Sunday, celebrates the Resurrected One who sends his people forth to homes and to parks, where the Galileans of today's world continue to relax, eat, and drink with Jesus, now the Risen Lord. This tangible experience of being loved, affirmed, and valued by our God, the God of all life, is the deepest affirmation of the divine status of our human existence. With Easter Sunday comes a period of ten days of fiestas for the city of San Antonio with parades, carnivals, crownings, and many special events. The cathedral is the geographical and cultural center of these celebrations; providing recreation, especially for the poor who cannot pay the entrance fee at theme parks, is part of its mission. The surrounding area is filled with the sounds of popular music, the smells of *tripitas*, hamburgers, tacos, enchiladas, fajitas, and cotton candy. People come to dance, to visit, to eat, and to meet friends. These festive gatherings seem an extension of the Eucharist. Is this not what Jesus was about? Was not his table fellowship a sign that the new creation had begun?

8

IMAGINING THE CITY OF GOD

Virgilio P. Elizondo

At the time of its origins, no one suspected that the small church of San Fernando would become the great meeting place of the two Americas. Located in the center of the city and also in the center of the two American continents, it serves as a spiritual and cultural crossroads of the peoples, cultures, and languages of the Americas. A prominent Latino cathedral in the United States, its most obvious characteristic is its spirit of welcoming everyone who enters as a child of God.

Today's modern city of San Antonio was originally laid out by the Spanish colonizers with its church and its plazas as the center of all life. The dome of the church marked the geographical center of the city. This was both practical and theological: practical, because the church was the tallest building; and theological, because God was understood as the center and source of all life. Everything radiated from the church and led to it, and this continuity between the secular and the sacred was natural for the community. Our Mexican ancestors celebrated their religious festivities in the streets and plazas while they celebrated civic events with tolling bells and religious ceremonies in the church.

Although San Fernando is very old and traditional, its sense of tradition does not represent a fixed or unchangeable way of doing things. Rather, it has a tradition of evolving creativity that depends on memory, faith, and imagination. In fidelity to the past, we freely interpret our beloved traditions in new and exciting ways, similar to the way we sing an old Mexican song to a modern Tejano tune. It is in and through this faithful creativity that the Spirit constantly breathes new life into San Fernando. Imagination and creativity

99

grounded in memory and fueled by the enthusiasm of faith are the very essence of the tradition of San Fernando.

The God of our ancestors, the God in whose image we have been created, is the God of imagination and creativity. The greatest triumph of God's imagination is the incarnation of God in the form of the Galilean Jesus of Nazareth, son of Mary and friend of publicans and sinners. God took on the flesh and personality of *mestizo* Galilee, commonly despised for its cultural mixture, and launched a new and universal unity within humanity.

The mystery of Jesus of Nazareth—from conception to glorification—soars beyond all the schemes of our limited human thought. Who would dare to imagine that the all-powerful Creator of heaven and earth would accompany us in our sorrowful, painful, scandalous, and often meaningless human lives? The liberating and illuminative power of Jesus is that he invited all people to see themselves in ways they had never before imagined. Those cast out by society could experience themselves as beloved children of God, and those who knew themselves as important and virtuous could see their limitations and sinfulness. The pastoral work of San Fernando is to recognize, appreciate, celebrate, and share the beauty, dignity, and potential of all people. This is at the very heart of our Christian faith. Part of the majestic beauty of San Fernando is that it does not seek to hide the scars and wounds and tears of our human condition.

THE GALILEAN IN OUR MIDST

What brings everything within San Fernando into harmonious unity and allows its ultimate meaning to be clearly seen and experienced is the centrality of the crucified victim, located just over the tabernacle. We know without doubt that the one the world crucified and killed, God raised. He is present among us today in the mystery of what we call "the real presence." His body on the cross reminds us to look at the hands and feet that were pierced by the nails for the sake of our salvation. Our risen crucified Lord communicates to us the power of endurance for the sake of others. Indeed, this is the light of the world, the only light that can lead us out of the darkness of selfishness.

As the mystery of the crucifixion illuminates humanity's darkness, so the crucified victim on the cross illuminates the entire cathedral and brings to light the goodness of the fallen and the sinfulness of the upright. From the cross, Christ brings to light the ultimate truth about men and women. From the first moment of entry into the church, it is the crucified that draws our attention. Under the cross we see either the celebration of the Eucharist or the presence of Christ in the tabernacle, just below the feet of the crucified. Jesus is always there for us, ready to listen, console, and accompany us in our struggles.

The Eucharist at San Fernando attracts people from all walks of life and from all ethnic and social backgrounds. There is no doubt, though, that the overwhelming majority of the people are from among the Latino poor of San Antonio. Like the majority of the followers of Jesus, they are the ones who most enjoy his table fellowship. Though their suffering is usually not concealed, it is surpassed by their joy of being together in the Lord's house.

Of those who enter this beautiful "home," most do not own their own homes, and some are homeless, but here they can enjoy the comfort and beauty they do not have at home. This challenges all of us to recognize the sacredness of people's homes and to work for better and more affordable housing. Similarly, many are functionally illiterate, and the Mass and sermon are the only education available to them. A lector who may be unemployed can stand proudly in a coat and tie and proclaim the reading of the day. This is his job. The prayers of the faithful often include *el llanto del pobre*—poor people asking that their water not be cut off, that their child be released from prison, or for help in arranging for Medicare. This is where we share each other's concerns. As we join hands for the Our Father, we energize one another, and we recognize that there is hope in our togetherness, which in a moment will be sealed with the body and blood of the Lord. We are affirmed and energized to move forward into something new.

The Eucharist is celebrated with great participation, popular song, visual imagery, and strong and clear-cut gospel preaching that sparks within everyone new possibilities of life. It is a continuation of the table fellowship of Jesus. The very context in which the liturgy is celebrated at San Fernando helps one to appreciate the personal and the collective, the earthly and the cosmic, the temporal and the eternal dimensions of the Eucharist.

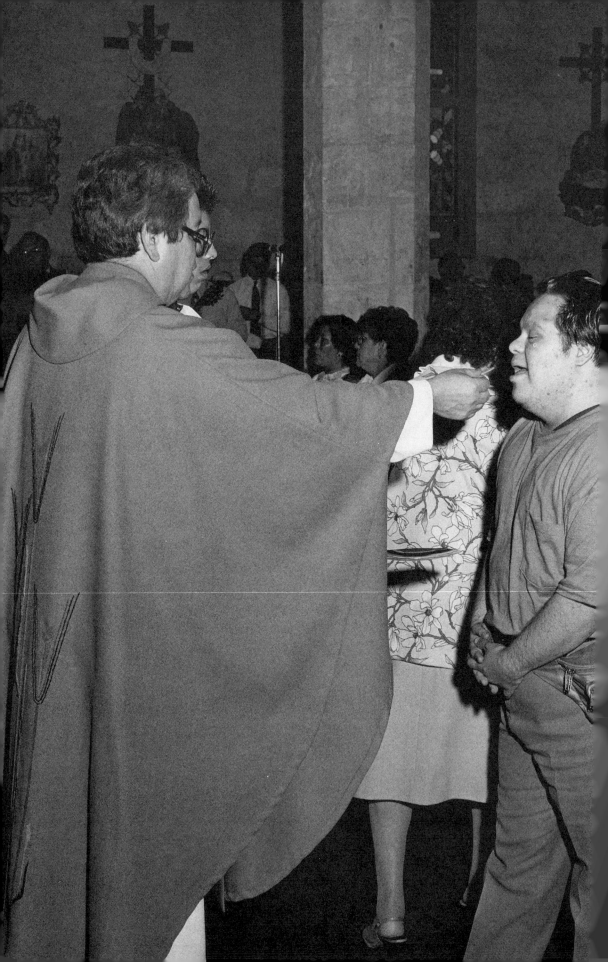

The Eucharist celebrates the ultimate *mestizaje*—the body and blood of the Divine Savior are given at the table for everyone so that all humanity might become one body and blood. All boundaries are broken in this great mystery of faith that has begun but is yet to come to completion. Rooted in the past, it moves into the future without hesitation, binding and blending together generations, languages, and traditions. Nothing truly human is alien to the sacredness of San Fernando.

AN EVOLVING RITUAL TRADITION

The work and struggles of the people of San Antonio have become the basis of new liturgical celebrations that have emerged at the cathedral. Indeed, this was true of the biblical experience, wherein the struggles for dignity, freedom, and life gave rise and shape to new celebrations. The calendar year at San Fernando is filled with such celebrations, and we anticipate that more will develop over the coming years.

January 15, the celebration of the *Cristo Negro de Esquipulas*, has become a very special day at San Fernando. This is also the birthday of Martin Luther King, Jr., and the Black Christ brings the suffering and struggles for freedom of other peoples onto center stage at San Fernando.

February 2, the feast of the Presentation, is a celebration of life and of the infinite value of each newborn. Parents with children who are one year or younger bring their babies to the cathedral to present them to the Lord. Pregnant mothers are blessed. A wreath of flowers is placed on the altar for those babies who have died in the womb. Another wreath is added for those who died during their first year of life. Finally, a woman dressed in black with her face covered places a wreath on the altar for the babies who were not allowed to be born. This symbolic gesture speaks more powerfully than any demonstration or angry words about the value of all human life.

In the middle of March, we celebrate the founding of the *villa* of San Antonio and the establishment of the parish of *Nuestra Señora de la Candelaria y Guadalupe*. The parish church, the original center of the city, continues to be the official center of San Antonio. The descendants of the immigrants from the Canary Islands celebrate with great pride the beginning of the city and parish.

The last week in April is Fiesta Week, a time when the entire city gathers to celebrate the beginning of modern-day Texas, with the cathedral at the center of the fiesta. The coronation of the *Rey Feo* (the ugly king) who reigns over Fiesta Week takes place at the cathedral. The person who raises the most money for scholarships to help the poor of San Antonio attend college is chosen king.

The month of May is packed with special celebrations, and the most popular is Mother's Day. Because we are a festive people, our liturgies center around what our hearts urge us to celebrate: the great gifts and marvels of God in the midst of our everyday lives. It is not surprising that Mother's Day has a very special place in our hearts. Our celebration begins with a joyous mariachi concert that is televised. During the Mother's Day Mass itself, poems, songs, and flowers are offered to the mothers, grandmothers, and mothers-to-be. As we promote the advancement of women in church and society, we emphasize the privilege, dignity, and responsibilities of motherhood.

The climax of the month of May is our city-wide graduation celebration, to which all high schools are invited to send three or four graduates in their caps and gowns. Teachers, administrators, and families join the students in thanking God for having arrived at this moment in their lives. All of San Antonio's graduates are symbolically present in this celebration that encourages others to complete their educations. One year the lessons were read by a mother graduating from college and her daughter who was graduating from high school.

June has one major celebration, Father's Day. We are convinced we need to give more value to full fatherhood, not just biological fatherhood, but fatherhood that persists through every step of a child's development. During the Mass we sing a song one of our local musicians has composed about his own father.

In July we celebrate the birthday of our country with a big Fourth of July Mass. We thank God for the true greatness of this country and also prophetically question the many abuses that still dominate it today. Then we celebrate French Day on the Sunday closest to July 14, thanking God for the principles of the French Revolution and for the contribution of French religious orders to the church in San Antonio—the colleges, the schools, the hospital, and the diocesan

structure. The physical structure of the nave dates from the period of French leadership during the nineteenth century.

The first Monday of August begins the annual month-long revival to bring lapsed Catholics back to the church. Begun in preparation for Pope John Paul II's visit to the cathedral in 1987, it commemorates that visit by inviting people back into full sacramental communion with the church. Around one hundred people attend three nights a week for four weeks. At the end of four weeks of basic instruction, we celebrate the sacraments.

August ends with a "Back to School Mass" for administrators and faculty from all schools—public and private. This is an opportunity to come together to pray for a good school year, with an emphasis on working together as parents, teachers, administrators, and churches for the betterment of all our children.

During September we celebrate our Mexican heritage. On the Sunday closest to September 16, we celebrate the *Diez y Seis* Mass in the style of a large Mexican fiesta with *charros, chinas poblanas*, mariachi music, and flags. The people respond enthusiastically to the playing and singing of traditional Mexican music. This day celebrates our declaration of independence from European colonizers and the moment when we assumed responsibility for our own lives.

September is also the time of our annual Health Fair when Mexican-American and other doctors of San Antonio transform the entire cathedral area into a massive popular clinic of free services. Doctors, nurses, health-care providers, and medical students gather together in the streets and plazas around San Fernando to be of service to the poor and the needy and to provide free medical examinations.

During September we also hold the annual Procession of Hope for persons with AIDS and their friends and families. This ecumenical event brings together people of all faiths to accompany and strengthen those afflicted with AIDS. This outreach takes us beyond our religious boundaries to the unity of a caring human family. The procession begins at the Alamo. As it approaches the cathedral, festive bells ring and San Fernando's parishioners sing *"De Colores"* while they welcome the procession with flowers. Even this small gesture of festive welcome to the cathedral begins a special type of healing.

During October we celebrate Pan-Americanism on the Sunday closest to October 12, praying for forgiveness for our sins against the native peoples and thanking God for the opportunities the Americas have offered to the poor and hopeless of the world. We also pray that our spirit of welcoming the tired and broken immigrants of the world might continue.

San Fernando also keeps alive its traditions and memory by naming and celebrating its saints. While we recognize that only the Holy See can officially name saints for the universal church, we recognize that people who have lived among us have shown an equally great and even heroic concern for the welfare of others. They are the people who have truly struggled and sacrificed to convert human society into the Kingdom of God. These people are our "local" saints.

On *El Día de los Muertos* (the Day of the Dead), the feast of the faithful departed, we honor and remember our dead so that they, in turn, continue to give us life. This liturgy brings together the Christian teaching of the communion of the saints and our ancient native belief that the ancestors are alive as long as we remember them. This is the day when the entire community remembers not only individual family members and friends, but also people whom we do not want to forget, the people who have allowed us to see the face and hear the voice of God present among us. The life stories and struggles of our local heroes are retold and gradually transformed into the myths of life, becoming part of our own saving history. This is the day when we are mystically united with our ancestors, our heroes, our prophets, our visionaries, and all those who are gradually forming us into the particular people that we are. This, then, is also the day when we reclaim the power to name our own heroes and saints. In creating our own pantheon of saints, those whose lives have become sacred to us, we formulate the image of the human beings we want to become, an expression of the ultimate freedom and affirmation of a people.

Very appropriately, the yearly celebrations of God's love climax with the celebration of the traditional U.S. feast of Thanksgiving at the end of November. This celebration of the past projects us into a totally new future.

UNITING THE CITY IN WORSHIP

In many places around the world, religion has the power to divide people and put them in opposition to one another. If it happened in

San Antonio or in the United States, it would be a disaster. We must dream, pray, and work so that religion unites people while respecting their differences. At San Fernando we have discovered that differences do not have to divide; quite the opposite. Through our life-journey of *mestizaje*, we have learned that they can enrich and open up new possibilities that have never before been imagined. We have discovered that by welcoming others while respecting their differences, we are indeed enriching one another.

Although San Fernando is very Mexican in tradition, it is definitely not anti-U.S.A. On the contrary, we appreciate the unlimited potential of our *mestizaje*. We recognize that new possibilities lie in front of us. What we most appreciate about the United States is the wisdom of its founders in establishing a law and spirit of religious tolerance. The true greatness and even sacredness of this country is precisely its willingness to welcome everyone, regardless of race, color, or creed, even though this is not always borne out in practice. San Fernando can help turn this dream into reality. After all, one purpose of worship is to dream of things that are not yet and to bring them into existence through prayer and ritual.

Today, tolerance is not enough. We must seek ways for people of the various religions to value each other, respect each other, work together, and most of all, pray together. We know that God is greater than any one expression—no matter how true it is—of God. The city of San Antonio includes Hispanics, Anglos, Asians, Africans, Native Americans; Catholics, Protestants, Orthodox, Fundamentalists, Jews, Muslims, Hindus, and Buddhists. Our Thanksgiving service brings together all of these groups in a previously unimagined prayerful and festive celebration of our differences.

Each religious leader is invited to offer a brief prayer from within his or her tradition. There is a Buddhist chant, a Muslim call to prayer, a Native American ritual dance with chants and drums, and an African-American gospel choir that joins with a mariachi choir to provide music. No sermon is necessary, for the very action of praying together is the most powerful sermon possible. Our Thanksgiving service brings all of us together in the historical and geographical God-center of San Antonio, showing that San Fernando functions not exclusively as a Catholic cathedral, but as a center of unity and harmony for all the God-loving people of San Antonio and beyond.

Using biblical images, two women testified to the power of participating in this multireligious celebration. An elderly Catholic woman who loves praying the rosary said, "Father, I have always loved the painting of the Last Supper, but today I had the impression that I was present at the Last Supper at the end of time, maybe even in heaven!" And a Jewish woman said, "I had the feeling that we were the people who were inside Noah's Ark, getting ready to begin the new creation."

Salvation history is the story of the unexpected interventions of God in the lives of people, and the saving process of humanity continues today. Special events of our lives, such as Thanksgiving, are brought into the life and celebrations of the church because they are manifestations of God's providence. God is truly present in every moment of our lives, and it is the role of the church to help people appreciate the presence of the Divine.

During the past few years, many significant events have been brought into the realm of the sacred within the walls of the cathedral. In 1990, as soldiers were preparing to depart for Iraq, an entire battalion from San Antonio came to the cathedral to invoke God's blessing and protection. Hundreds of soldiers of all religions and ethnic groups marched in combat fatigues into the church. At the end of the Mass, the entire congregation raised their hands over them in a collective blessing. This was an emotionally charged moment. At the end of the blessing, the soldiers marched out into the buses waiting to take them to the airfields for departure. Hundreds of people gathered outside the church to bid them farewell. Regardless of ideologies or even convictions about U.S. involvement in the Gulf War, the people of San Antonio were united in profound emotion of their own flesh and blood going off to war.

At another time, one of our San Antonians, Henry Cisneros, was named to the President's cabinet as Secretary of Housing and Urban Development. Henry and his family had often worshiped at San Fernando. The entire community, including elected officials, was invited for a prayerful send-off. At the end of the televised Mass, the entire congregation raised hands over him and pronounced a prayer of ordination to the ministry of public service, including the television audience of several million. This was a moving and meaningful expression of the baptismal priesthood of the people of God.

Similarly, when the popular candidate for the presidency of Mexico, Luis Donaldo Colosio, was assassinated, San Fernando, in cooperation with the Hispanic Chamber of Commerce, immediately organized a memorial Mass. Thorough press and television coverage in Mexico indicated that the people in Mexico were very impressed that such a ceremony would take place in the United States.

BEYOND CITY WALLS

The pastors of the original San Fernando would never have dreamed that one day the entire United States (and even beyond) would participate regularly in religious services at San Fernando. Yet for the last ten years San Fernando has reached out to shut-ins, the imprisoned, and to all those who cannot come to church through its televised Masses, visiting more parishioners each Sunday than any parish could manage in a lifetime.

Every Sunday morning people from the entire United States and much of the Americas, especially in Mexico and Canada, unite in prayer through the cathedral. Literally millions are praying together for one another, with each one praying for everyone, and everyone praying for each one. We become one heart and one mind through the message of the gospel proclaimed from San Fernando. Each day's mail brings letters from viewers, both Catholic and non-Catholic, from around the United States who affirm what our televised ministry means to them.

> It had been years since I had been to church, but through your TV Mass, I have returned to the church. (Jensen Beach, Florida)

> I am not a Catholic, but your program is the best thing on television. It has really taught me what real love is about. (Northridge, California)

> I am a minister of the United Church of Christ. Finding your Mass was a most welcome event. I know of many persons of different persuasions who find great benefit in it. I pray that you may continue and reach more and more. (Mobridge, South Dakota)

Your celebrations are so genuine that even though I am not a believer, I love to be with you every Sunday—you are the only real program left on television. (A self-proclaimed atheist from Pennsylvania)

It's truly like a forecast of heaven—if heaven is anything like your Sunday Mass, I can't wait to get there. (Boston)

Televised worship services from the cathedral do not highlight any particular priest or preacher or choir. Rather, it is the entire assembly—priests, choirs, and people—that takes the basic gospel message of the joy of radical acceptance, forgiveness, love, and fellowship to all viewers. The entire congregation participates in the message.

Today, the cathedral has a fully equipped studio run by a creative team of professional technicians. Via a microwave antenna on the roof of the cathedral, we can transmit any of our worship services directly to a television station for relay to a satellite and thus to the world. The parish of San Fernando, a parish made up mainly of poor people with limited financial resources, reaches an estimated audience of some ten million viewers each week. In addition to our regular Sunday Mass, we also televise special events such as the annual multireligious Thanksgiving service, the *serenata* to our Lady of Guadalupe, the *Dia de los Muertos* Mass, the concert of public school children, and—juxtaposed with the televised Way of the Cross led by the Pope—we produce a live broadcast of the annual Good Friday *Siete Palabras* special for Univision.

Viewers often telephone to talk, to ask for prayers, or to express their gratitude. A team of parishioners is trained to talk with anyone who calls. Nowadays, hardly a week goes by without a visit from some member of our television family. Indeed, this seems to be leading to a new and unsuspected phenomenon: San Antonio is now a destination of growing numbers of pilgrims from other states and countries who come precisely to participate in the Sunday Mass. Usually it is a natural phenomenon, an apparition of Mary, the presence of a pope, or a legend that attracts pilgrims. At San Fernando it is the Eucharist. People come precisely to participate physically in the family warmth and joy that they have discovered within our Catholic Mass.

THE PUBLIC WITNESS OF THE CONGREGATION

The religious traditions of the past that live in our collective memory and hearts and in our present experience teach that survival requires imagination and creativity. Faith, born of tradition, teaches a profound sense of gratitude for the infinite goodness of God and that life is a mystery to be loved, lived, and celebrated. It is this combination of memory, experience, and faith that forms our theology and gives rise to our vision, hope, and dreams.

The spiritual blessings we have received from so many diverse people lead us to rejoice and share our joy with others. From this joy come new ideas for a more loving and caring humanity. It is not by criticizing or castigating people that we call them to the fullness of their being, but by celebrating what has already begun in each one of them. As people cast off their fears, they strive toward the fullness of who they can be, and they begin to experience the true beauty and worth of others. Thus, we rejoice in our diversity, our *mestizaje*, because no one person, ethnicity, race, or religion can exhaust the beauty and grandeur of God. Only a God who is beyond all human barriers can lead us to transform our differences from sources of division to sources of enrichment. With San Fernando standing at the crossroads of histories, cultures, and frontiers, we seek to bring new life to our city and to humanity through the Reign of God as lived, proclaimed, and initiated by Jesus. This is the dream at San Fernando.

AFTERWORD: SOUL OF THE CITY

David P. García

Shortly after arriving as the new rector of San Fernando Cathedral I met Mario. I was immediately impressed with his friendliness, commitment, and ability to work with people. As I learned more about his story I began to better understand the special place that I had been called to serve.

Mario is a thirty-year-old cook at a local elementary school in San Antonio. He has been in this country since the age of seventeen and speaks English with difficulty. When he arrived in San Antonio he was undocumented and had a hard time finding stable work. He literally lived from day to day on whatever pay he could get from sporadic jobs. At one point, when the people he originally lived with lost patience with his lack of steady income, he was homeless for two days and slept under a bridge. Fortunately, some other friends from Mexico offered him a place and were willing to accept whatever he could pay them. Mario never intended to stay in the United States, only to make some money and return to have a better chance at beginning life in his home town. His story is typical of many who come to this country from Latin America.

Mario's friends took him to San Fernando Cathedral where they had been attending Mass for some time. The language and traditions reminded him of his childhood in Mexico. People welcomed him and offered help in finding a job and resolving problems. He was invited to join the choir. He had found a new family that made him feel wanted.

At San Fernando Mario had finally entered a community where he could both feel at home with the traditions he remembered from Mexico and at the same time begin to integrate more with the ways these traditions were evolving in a new context. As he became more involved in the parish, he was asked one December to play the role of Joseph in *la gran posada*, San Fernando's annual presentation in the streets of downtown San Antonio. The *posada* traces the journey of Joseph and Mary as they try to find shelter on the night of Christ's birth. Mario's shyness made him hesitant, but he was encouraged by others who had grown to admire him. He accepted the part and recalls that throughout the drama he felt different, as if he were someone else. He felt he was finally doing something for God, answering God's call, and he was proud of all that had happened. He put himself completely into the part. At that moment Mario was really not Mario, but José, the husband of the Virgin María. He forgot all his problems. He discovered something he did not know he had, the gift of committing himself to something completely. He didn't want it to end.

The part of Mary in *la gran posada* that year was played by Lupita, a young woman who had come to San Antonio from Mexico with her family. Lupita was also a member of the choir. In playing the roles of the man and woman who were to be the parents of Jesus, Mario and Lupita lived out the story of a young couple far from home, seeking a place to be welcomed so that they could await a new birth. As they walked the streets of the downtown historic center of the city with the San Fernando community and many others, they entered into a gospel story that was at once past and present. Something happened to them as it did to many others who allowed themselves to be part of that great public ritual. The story that is San Fernando continued to develop and work its mystery, dramatically impacting their lives.

Two years later Mario and Lupita married at San Fernando. They began to live out the reality of the story that had brought them together. They began the journey together to make a home for Christ, the Christ who would be seen in their commitment to each other and to their faith community. Steeped in the traditions they knew and loved so well, they were now carrying forth those traditions and adding to them by their life together and especially their continuing life at San Fernando.

Mario is now helping new stories happen. He directs the public drama of the Passion during Holy Week and helps organize *la gran posada* before Christmas. For three years Mario has directed the

Passion Play with the commitment and skill of a Hollywood director but with the soul of a true disciple. He has put together a drama that attracts more than 15,000 people to the downtown plaza in front of San Fernando. Local and out-of-town media crowd in to cover the event, and commentators call it one of the best presentations in the country of the Passion of Jesus.

Lupita has also changed dramatically. She is now the parish secretary and manages the front office with its numerous responsibilities. Her dedication to the parish and to the people who form this community carries forth the traditions of San Fernando in new and creative ways.

The Passion Play and San Fernando have transformed Mario and Lupita. These have brought out the best in them and have connected them ever more closely to the traditions of the church. They share their commitment with others who take part in the rituals, dramas, and events at San Fernando as well as the thousands of visitors who come each month to experience the mystery of entering into the gospel story.

Lupita and Mario are also beginning the age-old process that has kept San Fernando so alive for nearly three centuries. They are handing on their traditions to the next generation. Every year Lupita dresses up their three small children to be part of the Passion Play. As they walk along with their mother, who also takes a role, and as they see their father directing the play, the children are given a beautiful gift—the sacred customs of their ancestors. These children, as well as other children of San Fernando, are a pledge that the memories will continue to give life to this community for a long time to come.

Mario and Lupita are great examples of the power of San Fernando, a power that touches many people who allow themselves to be a part of its mystery. Through the traditions of public celebrations and rituals, the people are affirmed in who they are and are called to develop themselves to be the best they can be. Traditions are carried forward and celebrated in imaginative and creative ways. It is a thing of the heart. All who participate are touched in some way. Little by little they are drawn into the experience. At some point they realize that they are completely involved and it is now theirs. It does not belong only to the priests or special ministers of the church. It becomes personal. It becomes family. One is changed, drawn in, and asks, "What more can I do?"

Something is happening at San Fernando, though I am not sure what it is. Old traditions are being made new and different. We are taking beautiful ancient traditions and rituals—the Passion Play, *las posadas*, the Seven Last Words, the *pésame*, *Día de los Muertos*, *La Virgen de Guadalupe*, and *quinceañeras*—and we are rediscovering them with new imagination. The people are entering into them as old experiences that have been given a creative new life. Somehow we are doing more than we know, touching more than we will ever realize. It is an embracing reality, a living phenomenon. It is surely the work of God.

It has been my privilege to be rector of this cathedral community for three years. These years have been some of the hardest yet most fulfilling times of my life. After twenty-three years of priesthood I am also being touched anew in my commitment through the power of San Fernando. This special church has helped integrate, affirm, support, develop, challenge, and ground many generations of people in south Texas. They come to celebrate who they are, where they come from, and where they can go together in this faith community that has wielded such a remarkable influence over so many people in its 267 years of existence.

This is the ongoing story of a special community of faith. This is the continuing narrative of an ancient yet ever-new people who are touched and transformed by this place. I believe this mystery can be found wherever people are willing to remember, imagine, and create. That mystery certainly lives in this unique church, this living sacred space, this soul of the city.

Maybe Mario says it best each year to the players as they begin the rehearsals for the Passion Play, "Feel it, live it, enter."

FURTHER READING

Aquino, María Pilar. *Our Cry for Life: Feminist Theology from Latin America.* Maryknoll, NY: Orbis Books, 1993.

Bass, Dorothy C., ed. *Practicing Our Faith: A Way of Life for a Searching People.* San Francisco: Jossey-Bass, 1997.

Boff, Leonardo and Virgilio Elizondo, eds. *1492-1992: The Voice of the Victims.* London: SCM Press, 1990.

Duby, Georges. *The Age of the Cathedrals: Art and Society, 980-1420.* Chicago: University of Chicago Press, 1981.

Elizondo, Virgilio P. *The Future Is Mestizo: Life Where Cultures Meet.* New York: Crossroad, 1992.

————. *Galilean Journey: The Mexican-American Promise.* Maryknoll, NY: Orbis Books, 1983.

————. *Guadalupe: Mother of the New Creation.* Maryknoll, NY: Orbis Books, 1997.

————. "Hispanic Theology and Popular Piety: From Interreligious Encounter to a New Ecumenism." *Catholic Theological Society of American Proceedings* 48 (1993): 1-14.

————. *La Morenita: Evangelizer of the Americas.* San Antonio: Mexican American Cultural Center Press, 1980.

Elizondo, Virgilio P. and Sean Freyne, eds. *Pilgrimage.* Maryknoll, NY: Orbis Books, 1996.

Elizondo, Virgilio P. and Timothy M. Matovina. *Mestizo Worship: A Pastoral Approach to Liturgical Ministry.* Collegeville, MN: Liturgical Press, 1998.

Espín, Orlando O. *The Faith of the People: Theological Reflections on Popular Catholicism.* Maryknoll, NY: Orbis Books, 1997.

Francis, Mark R. and Arturo J. Pérez-Rodríguez. *Primero Dios: Hispanic Liturgical Resource.* Archdiocese of Chicago: Liturgy Training Publications, 1997.

García, David. "*Las Posadas*: The Power of Processions." *Church* (forthcoming).

————. "Processions: The Soul of the City." *Modern Liturgy* 25 (November 1998).

————. "Sacramental Preparation: A Mission Model." *Church* (Fall 1997): 31-32.

————. "La Semana Santa en San Fernando." *Gracias!* (forthcoming).

García-Rivera, Alex. *The Community of the Beautiful: A Theological Aesthetics.* Collegeville, MN: Liturgical Press (forthcoming).

———. "Mass Should Be a Come-as-You-Are Party." *U.S. Catholic* (August 1995): 32-34.

———. *St. Martín de Porres: The "Little Stories" and the Semiotics of Culture.* Maryknoll, NY: Orbis Books, 1995.

Goizueta, Roberto. S. *Caminemos con Jesús: Toward a Hispanic/Latino Theology of Accompaniment.* Maryknoll, NY: Orbis Books, 1995.

———. "San Fernando Cathedral: Incarnating the Theology Born of the Mexican American Cultural Center." *Listening: Journal of Religion and Culture* 32 (Fall 1997): 190-203.

Isasi-Díaz, Ada María and Yolanda Tarango. *Hispanic Women: Prophetic Voice in the Church.* San Francisco: Harper & Row, 1988; reprint, Minneapolis: Fortress Press, 1992.

Journal of Hispanic/Latino Theology. Especially the August 1997 issue, a special issue on Our Lady of Guadalupe edited by Virgilio P. Elizondo and Timothy M. Matovina.

Matovina, Timothy M. "Guadalupan Devotion in a Borderlands Community." *Journal of Hispanic/Latino Theology* 4 (August 1996): 6-26.

———. "Sacred Place and Collective Memory: San Fernando Cathedral, San Antonio, Texas." *U.S. Catholic Historian* 15 (Winter 1997): 33-50.

———. "San Fernando Cathedral and the Alamo: Sacred Place, Public Ritual, and Construction of Meaning." *Journal of Ritual Studies* (forthcoming).

———. *Tejano Religion and Ethnicity: San Antonio, 1821-1860.* Austin: University of Texas Press, 1995.

Rodriguez, Jeanette. *Our Lady of Guadalupe: Faith and Empowerment among Mexican-American Women.* Austin: University of Texas Press, 1994.

Wind, James P. *Places of Worship: Exploring Their History.* Nashville: American Association for State and Local History, 1990.

Wind, James P. and James W. Lewis, eds. *American Congregations.* Chicago: University of Chicago Press, 1994, 2 volumes.

PHOTO CREDITS

VIDEO—SOUL OF THE CITY

Learn more about what an urban cathedral can be in a modern city in this "video painting" that focuses on Holy Week worship and rituals at San Fernando Cathedral.

> "Soul of the City" shows how Bible, life, culture, and liturgy all come together. [It presents] an image of the immense contribution that Hispanic popular religion has to make to the pastoral evolution of the church in North America.
> —Rev. Paul Philibert, O.P., Director,
> Notre Dame Institute for Church Life

Produced by Adán M. Medrano and directed by Gerardo Rueda, this 28-minute video is intended for use in the classroom to understand liturgy and public ritual, methods of parish ministry and parish renewal, and also for study groups during Lent or Holy Week. A study guide is included.

The video may be ordered for $29.95 plus $3.00 shipping/handling from:

JM Communications
3701 Kirby Drive, Suite 834
Houston, Texas 77098
Tel: (713) 524-1382
Fax: (713) 524-1383
http://www.jmcommunications.com

About the Authors

Virgilio P. Elizondo, *(right)* a native of San Antonio and former rector of San Fernando Cathedral, is director of Archdiocesan Television Ministry for San Antonio. He is also a board member of *Concilium,* the international Catholic journal, and the author of many books, including *Guadalupe: Mother of the New Creation* and *Galilean Journey: The Mexican-American Promise* (Orbis Books).

Timothy M. Matovina is assistant professor of theology at Loyola Marymount University in Los Angeles. The book review editor of the *Journal of Hispanic/Latino Theology,* he is author of numerous articles and five books, including *Tejano Religion and Ethnicity: San Antonio, 1821-1860* and *The Alamo Remembered: Tejano Accounts and Perspectives* (University of Texas Press).